SpringerBriefs in Economics

Development Bank of Japan Research Series

This series is characterized by the close academic cohesion of financial economics, environmental economics, and accounting, which are the three major fields of research of the Research Institute of Capital Formation (RICF) at the Development Bank of Japan (DBJ). Readers can acquaint themselves with how a financial intermediary efficiently restructuring firms in financial distress, can contribute to economic development.

The aforementioned three research fields are closely connected with one another in the following ways. DBJ has already developed several corporation-rating methods, including the environmental rating by which DBJ decides whether or not to make concessions to the candidate firm. To evaluate the relevance of this rating, research, which deploys not only financial economics but also environmental economics, is necessary.

The accounting section intensively studies the structure of IFRS and Integrated Reporting to predict their effects on Japanese corporate governance. Although the discipline of accounting is usually isolated from financial economics, structural and reliable prediction is never achieved without sufficient and integrated knowledge in both fields.

Finally, the environmental economics section is linked to the accounting section in the following manner. To establish green accounting (environmental accounting), it is indispensable to explore what the crucial factors for the preservation of environment (e.g. emission control) are. RICF is well-equipped to address the acute necessity for discourse among researchers who belong to these three different fields.

More information about this series at http://www.springer.com/series/13542

Kozo Horiuchi · Masayuki Otaki

Dr. Osamu Shimomura's Legacy and the Postwar Japanese Economy

DBJ

Springer

Kozo Horiuchi
Hosei University
Tokyo
Japan

and

Research Institute of Capital Formation
Development Bank of Japan
Tokyo
Japan

Masayuki Otaki
Institute of Social Science
The University of Tokyo
Tokyo
Japan

and

Research Institute of Capital Formation
Development Bank of Japan
Tokyo
Japan

ISSN 2191-5504 ISSN 2191-5512 (electronic)
SpringerBriefs in Economics
ISSN 2367-0967 ISSN 2367-0975 (electronic)
Development Bank of Japan Research Series
ISBN 978-981-10-5761-8 ISBN 978-981-10-5762-5 (eBook)
DOI 10.1007/978-981-10-5762-5

Library of Congress Control Number: 2017946947

Printed on acid-free paper

This Springer imprint is published by Springer Nature
The registered company is Springer Nature Singapore Pte Ltd.
The registered company address is: 152 Beach Road, #21-01/04 Gateway East, Singapore 189721, Singapore

IN MEMORIAM
Osamu Shimomura, 1910–1989
A Leading Economist: His Theory, Insight, and Determination

Contents

About the Authors

Kozo Horiuchi is a professor emeritus, Hosei University, Tokyo, Japan. He received his B.A. from the Department of Commerce, Hitotsubashi University in 1968. He then joined the Development Bank of Japan and received his M.A. from the Graduate School of Johns Hopkins University in 1973. Returning from the USA, he served as a research officer before becoming Chief Economist at the Research Institute of Capital Formation, DBJ. He received his Doctor of Business Administration from Hosei in 2008. While teaching at Hosei, he also studied at the Beijer Institute, the Royal Swedish Academy of Sciences.

Masayuki Otaki is a professor of economics at the University of Tokyo Institute of Social Science, and academic advisor at the Research Institute of Capital Formation, Development Bank of Japan. His main areas of research are macroeconomic theory, environmental economics, educational economics, and economic thought. Born in 1957, Prof. Otaki received a Bachelor's degree in economics from the University of Tokyo in 1981 and a Ph.D. in economics from the University of Tokyo in 1990. He was appointed professor of economics at the University of Tokyo Institute of Social Science in 2001.

Chapter 1
Introduction

Abstract In this book, we attempt to review the vision, theory, and policy of Dr. Osamu Shimomura (1910–1989). In addition, we try to analyze the historical development of the Japanese economy, examine the current economic problems, and give an outline of a new vision for the twenty first century. We look at the historical developments after World War II and discuss how to live in a "zero growth" economy. We conclude that a vision is essential for stability and sustainability of the market economy. We also learn precious lessons from studying the works of Dr. Shimomura.

Keywords High growth · National income doubling plan · Zero growth · Vision · Discipline

This book consists of two parts. In Part I, we will discuss the vision, theory, and policy of Dr. Shimomura related to the era of high growth and "zero growth." In Part II, we will try to clarify the implications of a "zero growth" vision and analyze problems such as "lost decades," sustainability, and corporate management.

(Part I)

Seventy years have passed since World War II ended in 1945. During this period, Japan's economy experienced significant changes. The postwar history of the Japanese economy may be divided into three periods.

Chapter 2 summarizes the economic situation in Japan after the war. The first 10 years of the postwar period, from 1945 to 1954, is called the era of "reconstruction or rehabilitation," during which the Japanese economy recovered from the ruin of war. During this period, the government policy prioritized controlling severe inflation and increasing industrial production. These two objectives were difficult to attain in the midst of economic disorder. At that time, the Japanese economy was compared to a boat sailing in a turbulent sea.

In Chap. 3, we discuss high growth. The second postwar period spanning 19 years, from 1955 to 1973, was an era of high (rapid) economic growth. The Japanese economy continued to grow 10% annually and it was on a balanced

K. Horiuchi and M. Otaki, *Dr. Osamu Shimomura's Legacy and the Postwar Japanese Economy*, Development Bank of Japan Research Series,
DOI 10.1007/978-981-10-5762-5_1

growth path. In 1960, Dr. Shimomura presented the vision of high economic growth. The government implemented active growth-oriented policies and set the economy on a high growth rate. As these economic policies had the effect of achieving rapid growth, a new economic vision prevailed among the Japanese people. This growth period is well known as Japanese economic miracle. Today, the people of Japan long for this buoyant economic period and refer to it as "the good old Showa."

Around 1970, the Japanese economy caught up with those of more advanced countries in Europe and entered a new phase of economic slowdown. This process is called "transformation from rapid growth to decelerating growth," but the oil crisis in 1973 disrupted the transitional process.

Chapter 4 discusses the "zero growth" period. The third postwar period comprising 42 years, from 1974 to 2015, was an era of low growth or "zero growth." After the oil crisis, the Japanese economy entered a new phase. Natural resources are not limitless. One of the key factors—an abundant supply of oil—which supported growth of the world economy was severely damaged. Japan lacked a clear economic vision. The economic progress was derailed and has been in serious disequilibrium. Since 1990, in particular, Japan has been continually witnessing a very low rate of economic growth. The term "lost decades" still prevails. People in politics and business are discussing how to get out of stagnant economy and propose several measures for economic growth.

The "zero growth" stage is a vision that was expressed by Dr. Shimomura when the first oil crisis broke out in 1973. A majority of economists and businesspersons criticized that a long-term forecast of "zero growth" was too pessimistic and insisted that Dr. Shimomura's prediction was flawed. We will see in this book that he was right. Today, some economists have began to predict a steady and sustainable economic future for Japan, which Dr. Shimomura implied in his vision of "zero growth" almost 40 years ago.

(Part II)

In Part II, we will try to extend further what "zero growth" vision implies in the twenty first century. The three subjects that we choose are current zero growth, sustainability, and corporate management.

Chapter 5 considers the economic factors that have contributed toward stagnancy in the Japanese economy. Since the 1990s, the Japanese economy has been experiencing "zero growth" as per Dr. Shimomura. This phase is being referred to as the 'lost decades' by the Japanese people. In this context, we focus on the following three factors: surge in foreign direct investment (FDI), enlarged aggregate demand management policy of the government, and serious digression of managerial skills.

First, a surge in FDI causes industrial hollowing, which may threaten employment and macroeconomic stability. Second, public debt has been accumulating rapidly since the beginning of the century. The current expansionary fiscal and monetary policies are unsustainable. In addition, the growth-oriented industrial policy based on neo-liberalism resulted in poor records. For example, the deregulation of the labor market stimulated FDI. Firms may increase efficiency through FDI. However, it does not necessarily prove that the economy as a whole would stay stable in a zero growth economy. Third, is a problem of serious digression of managerial skills. One of the reasons behind economic stagnancy is the deregulation of the labor market. This causes the meltdown of a firm as an organic entity through coordination failure. Supply side becomes inefficient and the Japanese economy has been sluggish.

A slowdown in productivity due to loss of organic structure of a firm and rapid accumulation of public debt ensue, which ultimately impact the Japanese economy in the long run.

Chapter 6 discusses changes in corporate management in the future to meet a vision of zero growth. On a microeconomic level, a vision of rapid growth of individual firms was formed in the 1960s. A growth-oriented business culture became common. The familiar Japanese business practices like competitive strategies for managing stakeholders, such as employees and suppliers, were strengthened.

It is useful to examine the relationship between the management of firms and the business environment to develop a vision of the corporation. Environmental management by firms is changing. It was "reactive" in the 1960s, which changed to "preventive" in the 1980s, and has been "strategic" since the 1990s. Corporate social responsibility (CSR) was first discussed in the 1970s, and this issue has been attracting attention again in recent years.

After the oil crisis, Japanese firms lost their vision. Several firms are still holding on to the business culture that prevailed in the growth period of the 1960s. It is difficult to change business culture in the short-term. However, leading corporations are aware of the global environmental problems, and have started to direct management strategy toward achieving social sustainability. CSR and stakeholder management are becoming increasingly important, thereby resulting in the emergence of a new vision of the corporation.

1.1 Economics of Shimomura: Shimomura Theory, High Growth, and Zero Growth

Dr. Shimomura is well known in Japan. He was the first economist who discovered that the Japanese economy would realize high (rapid) growth in the 1960s. He also proposed that the government should take very positive fiscal and monetary policies to attain high economic growth in Japan. He was one of the private members who assisted Prime Minister Hayato Ikeda and contributed significantly toward the framing of the National Income Doubling Plan (1960–1970) of the government.

The high economic growth policy of the Ikeda administration was successful and the Japanese economy began to grow very rapidly. People felt as if they were driving over the new expressway. The vision, theory, and policy of Dr. Shimomura encouraged Japanese who had lost confidence after World War II. People were zealous for economic expansion as if they were participating in "economic Olympics." They were interested to see Japanese economy catching up with economies of the West.

The first oil crisis broke out in 1973. Dr. Shimomura dramatically changed his vision of the Japanese economy immediately after the crisis. He asserted that the high growth period was over and the Japanese economy would be forced to divert discontinuously into a "zero growth" (a very low growth) trajectory. He argued that economic agents, such as consumers, labor unions, corporate managers, banks, and the government, should exercise moderation and keep their own disciplines in the "zero growth" era.

In the era of great transition from high growth to "zero growth," the principle of laissez-faire would not guide the real economy to a stable and equilibrium state. The economic agents should observe discipline by considering the whole and exercising self-restraint. Dr. Shimomura emphasized that discipline on the part of major economic players was critically important. Discipline is a code of conduct that must be adopted during an era of "zero growth," and has a lot in common with "sympathy," which A. Smith emphasized.

Currently, the Japanese economy as a whole is not on the right track. The fundamental issue is a lack of a holistic vision of the economy and the corporation. Regrettably, economic agents neglected the warnings of Dr. Shimomura. The Japanese economy is in a state of serious disequilibrium. Dr. Shimomura passed away in 1989. Since then, for more than a quarter of a century, the Japanese economy has been unstable and stagnant. This scenario will be analyzed closely by referring to the "zero growth" vision.

1.2 Career of Dr. Shimomura

Dr. Shimomura was a descendant of the Samurai family. It is said that he was proud of one of the oldest ancestors who served a lord of the Saga clan as a chief retainer. Dr. Shimomura's motto was, "the mind should bear no evil thoughts." He had a strong propensity to serve the public. He was a temperate man and liked to have an independent view as an economist. He was also very logical and preferred to argue with other economists.

He studied economics at the Tokyo Imperial University. At that time, the Japanese economy was highly influenced by the Great Depression. He thought economics could help people in hardship. However, the Marxian economic teachings in the university made him realize that economics was not beneficial for finding ways to overcome severe depression. Concerning the period after the completion of his studies, it is believed that he was advised to continue with his studies and become a scholar at the university. However, he decided to work for the Ministry of Finance in 1934.

He was sent to New York in 1936, as a practice of the Ministry of Finance. At this time he obtained the first edition of *The General Theory* by J.M. Keynes. At that time, he had expressed difficulty in understanding Keynes' work thoroughly. However, apparently, it was a turning point for his understanding of macroeconomics. The theory of effective demand and multiplier effect constitutes a key element of the Shimomura theory.

In a wartime-controlled economy, Dr. Shimomura was engaged in deciding the wages and salaries of workers and executives of private corporations. This was a very strict incomes policy to control prices. Based on this experience, he was convinced that a controlled economy does not work well.

Immediately after the war, aggregate demand exceeded aggregate supply in Japan. As a government officer, he had to cope with soaring inflation. His economic policy was not aimed at suppressing aggregate demand but at increasing aggregate supply. His favorable mindset toward economic expansion led to the development of a high growth policy in the 1960s. Despite being a government officer, he trusted the free activities undertaken by the private entrepreneurs.

Concerning the research conducted as the economist, in 1951, Shimomura (1951) completed a theoretical paper on economic fluctuation and growth, following the works of P.A. Samuelson, R.F. Harrod, and J.A. Schumpeter. This thesis formed the basis for the Shimomura theory. Later, he received a doctor's degree for his research on the subject. He became well known in the professional academic circle. In 1953, he was appointed as a member of the monetary policy committee of the Bank of Japan while representing the Ministry of Finance.

In 1958, as an economist of the Ministry of Finance, he published a famous paper to realize the economic growth in Japan. In the postwar Japanese economy, aggregate demand had exceeded aggregate supply. However, he had recognized that the aggregate supply would tend to exceed aggregate demand around the end of 1950s. It was a historically important turning point for the Japanese economy. He insisted strongly that the government should reduce tax and increase expenditure to increase aggregate demand. He published a crucial paper that gave birth to The National Income Doubling Plan of Prime Minister Ikeda in 1960.

In 1960, he was appointed as a member of the executive board of the Japan Development Bank (JDB), and, in 1966, he became the first director of the Research Institute of Capital Formation (RICF) of JDB. He was active in economic analysis and forecasts throughout his lifetime. The Japanese entrepreneurs held Dr. Shimomura in high regard, and paid attention to and appreciated his unique view.

Several people referred to Dr. Shimomura and his works. Professor H. Uzawa had an opportunity to study under Professor N. Kaldor, one of the leading disciples of J.M. Keyens. According to Uzawa (1991), Kaldor and Shimomura had one thing in common. They used a simple number to express the core of economic analysis. In case of Dr. Shimomura, as we will see later, the output-capital ratio of the Japanese economy was 1, and the annual rate of economic growth was 10% in the 1960s and "zero" % after 1973. However, Uzawa pointed out that Shimomura was different from Kaldor in having a sharp intuition in macro economy, which was demonstrated in the famous growth controversy in 1959.

Dr. Shimomura was well known in Japan as an economist who formulated policies for high growth. He was a charismatic figure. Contrarily, he was almost unknown abroad. However, there is one exception. Hedberg, a Swedish journalist, wrote in his book *the Japanese Challenge* (1969) that Dr. Shimomura was a strong candidate for the Nobel Prize for Economics in the 1970s.

In his life, Dr. Shimomura published 10 books. He also published many written materials, such as papers for publication in economic journals; transcriptions of lectures, talks, and debates with economists; and interviews by journalists, which in total amounted to approximately 1150.

In this book, we will summarize Dr. Shimomura's work and analyze the major issues of the Japanese economy, including the current problem of stagnancy in the economy.

Dr. Shimomura, an architect of The National Income Doubling Plan in 1960, developed two visions of the Japanese economy: high growth in the 1960s and "zero growth" after the oil crisis in 1973. Based on Dr. Shimomura's theory of economic growth, we will understand that his vision of "zero growth" had profound implications for the sustainable development of macro economy and new management systems for the corporation in the twenty first century.

The vision of zero growth is closely linked with the new vision of the corporation, which will be successfully established as a "visionary company." In fact, a new type of corporate management is required and is emerging in Japan to meet the need of the hour. The proper management of social common capital, which Professor Uzawa theorized, and the adoption of the vision of zero growth will lead our market economy to the "stationary state" of J.S. Mill.

In the Research Institute of Capital Formation (RICF), a researcher usually becomes aware of Dr. Shimomura, the first director of the Institute, and shows academic interest in his work. This is a long-held trend and comprises a kind of implicit organizational culture of RICF.

We once undertook research at the RICF and received valuable lessons from Dr. Shimomura directly and indirectly. We were fortunate in having such a wonderful opportunity. We owe a debt of gratitude to our professors. We particularly thank late Hirofumi Uzawa for the concept of liberal society and theory of social common capital, Tadao Miyakawa for corporate management and corporate social responsibility (CSR), and Karl-Göran Mäler for environmental economics. We have benefited from the support of Yasutami Shimomura who kindly offered us less-discussed papers and photos of Dr. Shimomura. We appreciate the long run friendship at RICF with Hisashi Yaginuma, Morio Kuninori, Kimiko Hanabusa. We are grateful to intensive discussion with staffs of RICF. Especially, the warm kindness of Katsuhisa Uchiyama and Yuko Hosoda developed and furnished this book. Otaki was supported by JSPS KAKENHI Grant Number 17K03618.

References

Hedberg, H. H. (1969). *The Japanese challenge*. Stockholm: Bonniers.
Shimomura, O. (1951). Economic fluctuation and multiplier analysis. *Tokyo: Monthly Research Report, 40*(3), 61–89; *40*(5), 56–79; *40*(7), 1–86. Ministry of Finance (in Japanese).
Uzawa, H. (1991). In memory of Shimomura-san. In Compilation committee in honor of Dr. Shimomura (Ed.), *Osamu Shimomura* (in Japanese).

Part I
Vision, Theory, and Policy: High Growth and Zero Growth

Chapter 2
Postwar Reconstruction

Abstract The Japanese economy was severely damaged by the World War II. Production dropped to 30% of the pre-war peak. There were three serious problems when the war ended in 1945, namely unemployment, energy shortage, and inflation. This chapter focuses on the galloping inflation and analyzes how to control it. The government invoked the Emergency Financial Measures Order and enforced the price control order in 1946. As a government officer, Dr. Shimomura was responsible for checking inflation. He thought that the measures taken in 1946 were temporal and production recovery was fundamentally necessary. It was very difficult to increase production and to curb inflation at the same time. However, the government implemented an industrial policy called the Priority Production System, which opened the route to attain both the objectives successfully. Dr. Shimomura suffered from recurrence of lung disease in 1948 during his course of service with a government organization, forcing him to take a long leave. While bedridden, he started to write a thesis and completed it in 1951; the paper was titled *Economic Fluctuation and Economic Analysis*. In this paper, which depicts the "Shimomura theory," he developed the dynamics of Keynes theory and received a doctoral degree.

Keywords Inflation · Gradual approach · Priority production system · Economic growth · Shimomura theory

In this chapter, we will focus on postwar reconstruction and analyze how the Japanese economy contained inflation, rehabilitated industrial production, restored the trade balance, and attained economic autonomy without the US aid and Korean War special procurement policies. During this period, the Japanese economy faced very difficult problems that are beyond imagination. People had sincere policy debates on how to reconstruct Japanese economy. Economic base was very weak due to the damages caused by war, and mistakes in policy were not allowed. Economic policy played a very important role in enabling the Japanese economy to establish stability and order from the postwar confusions and ruins. Economic

K. Horiuchi and M. Otaki, *Dr. Osamu Shimomura's Legacy and the Postwar Japanese Economy*, Development Bank of Japan Research Series,
DOI 10.1007/978-981-10-5762-5_2

policy debates at that time had a very significant implication for high growth policy proposed in the 1960s.

During the reconstruction period, Dr. Shimomura took charge of the price stabilization policy of the government and worked towards formulating concrete measures for curbing inflation. In 1951, he completed a doctoral dissertation, *Economic Fluctuation and Multiplier Analysis*, in which he clarified the Shimomura theory. Dr. Shimomura applied his theory to the Japanese economy in the second half of 1950s. He successfully developed a high growth theory and proposed to the government the bold economic policy for Japan in the 1960s. The reconstruction period was a preparatory period for him to flourish as an active economist.

2.1 Economic Situation During the Reconstruction Period

The Japanese economy was severely damaged when the World War II ended in 1945. According to Kosai (1981), mining and industrial production in 1946 dropped to almost 30% of the prewar peak in 1934–1936 (see Table 2.1). In the first issue of *White paper on the Japanese Economy,* in 1947, Shimomura (1947, 1974) wrote a famous phrase, "a household is in the red. A firm is in the red. The government is in the red."

Nakamura (1981) pointed out three serious problems that the Japanese economy faced—unemployment, energy shortage, and inflation.

First, unemployment became a serious issue. The standard of living of city dwellers was low and cities were crowded with job seekers. People who failed to get jobs returned to their farm villages or became black marketeers. It implies that people did their best to earn a living. Therefore, the unemployment issue did not attract much attention; however, people faced discontentment. The problem of potential underemployment became apparent. Income difference of workers between large firms and small firms began to widen. The dual structure issue attracted attention of scholars and journalists. This unsatisfactory situation was

Table 2.1 Trends of economic indicators (1934–1936 = 100)

	1946	1950	1951	1952	1953
Real gross national product	61.6	64.7	99.0	110.6	119.1
Mining and industrial production	27.9	73.3	100.0	108.1	131.4
Production of primary industry	77.9	99.8	108.2	117.3	105.9
Volume of export	7.4[a]	32.0	35.8	35.8	37.7
Volume of import	20.8[a]	37.1	55.3	56.0	77.4
Consumption level	–	–	83.7	95.3	106.0
Real wage	30.2[b]	85.5	92.2	100.0	107.5

Note Primary industry (agriculture, forestry, and fisheries) [a]1948, [b]1947
Source Kosai (1981)

systematically solved during the course of time by realizing high growth in the 1960s.

Second, there was a shortage in resources. Japan was under economic blockade of the Allied Powers. The import of raw materials and oil was severely restricted. Energy, especially oil, was limited in supply, and hence it was difficult to resume production. Instead of oil, coal became the domestic source of energy that was used to increase industrial production.

Third, the inflation started galloping, thereby causing serious problem. People held a large amount of financial assets, such as deposits and public bonds. They had accumulated these assets during the war because they could not get what they wanted. They had enough purchasing power. Pent-up demand existed among the Japanese population, however, production decreased dramatically in 1946. The supply failed to meet the demand. This resulted in a typical demand-pull inflation.

2.2 Policy for Controlling Inflation

People were suffering from discontentment and depression. Checking inflation and resuming production and economic order formed the priorities of the government.

At first, the government prioritized controlling the galloping inflation. In February 1946, the government invoked the Emergency Financial Measures Order (*Kinyu Kinkyu Sochirei*), which required people to deposit all their cash in financial institutions and it set an upper limit on withdrawals for daily expenses by households. The Emergency Financial Measures Order was a firm resolution expressed by the government to restore monetary value and order. It was not possible to solve inflation problem only through the Emergency Financial Measures Order. However, it controlled the unlimited spread of speculative activities, and the Japanese economy could avoid hyperinflation like in the case of Germany after World War I.

Dr. Shimomura (1974) was convinced that the effect of Emergency Financial Measures Order on checking inflation could be realized by invoking the order only once. The government should not invoke the measures more than once. Therefore, in addition to the policy of freezing all deposits, another policy was the need of the hour. In March 1946, the government enforced the price control order. While deciding the price structure, it was decided to keep wages at the subsistence level of a household and official prices were determined by adding up costs. The official consumer prices were set below costs, with the result that production subsidies were necessary to compensate the loss of a firm, that is, price-difference subsidies. As a result, the real wage was determined in such a way that it was equal to the productivity at that time. However, people were not satisfied with low real wages and the standard of living, which was 30% of the prewar level. The government had to spend a variety of subsidies to maintain official prices. As a result, the fiscal balance became in the red.

Price control was to curb an increase of prices through the price-difference subsidies. Consumer prices were kept below the costs. Immediately after the war, the main objective of the government was to increase goods and supplies, which were sold and rationed at official prices, and to eliminate the black market economy. This policy was expected to increase the incentive to maintain current nominal wage. The government aimed at normalizing the distribution mechanism to restore market order and contain inflation.

However, Dr. Shimomura (1947) had a different view. In the context of that period, he thought that, even if inflation were controlled, people would not be satisfied with a very low standard of living. He admitted that price control was a temporary measure that was aimed at gaining time. He insisted that priority should be given to policies that can bring about production recovery and as a result satisfy people to a certain extent. This initiative would render the policy for curbing inflation effective and facilitate complete containment of inflation. Until then, vicious cycle between wages and prices would persist. Shimomura expected this way.

There was another issue. Economists and scholars had a view that inflation was caused by excess demand over supply, that is, demand-pull inflation. Therefore, they thought that the price increase preceded wage increase. However, Dr. Shimomura had a different view.[1] Due to the postwar labor reforms, labor unions had become very aggressive and demanded higher wages. Dr. Shimomura pointed at the possibility of wage increase as a cause of inflation and was very concerned with cost-push inflation. His idea of cost-push inflation was very original at that time.[2]

Production recovery leads to an increase in real wage or standard of living, a decrease in the difference of prices between official market and black market, and a decline in the price-difference subsidy, and these factors eventually contribute toward controlling inflation. In 1947 and 1948, there was an unanticipated recovery in industrial production, primarily due to the Priority Production System (*Keisha Seisan Hoshiki*). The Priority Production System was an industrial policy by the government, which aimed at industrial rehabilitation. This system placed highest priority on increasing the production of coal, which was the main domestic source of energy. Subsequently, the increased coal production was put into the iron and steel industry. Steel products were channeled into other basic industries, such as shipbuilding and electricity. In this manner, the Priority Production System realized an overall industry recovery.[3]

---

[1]When Dr. Shimomura planned economic policies, he collected statistical data fully, studied them carefully, and judged the actual economic situation. He seldom depended on a standard textbook of American Economics or the remarks of a man of authority. This partly explains why he had many serious controversies with economists and scholars.

[2]Three major reforms to democratize Japan were put into practice by the Allied Powers, in reality, the US forces. They were the dissolution of the *Zaibatsu*, land reform, and legalized labor union activities.

[3]The standard analysis emphasizes that the Priority Production System became the new source of inflation. A Marxian economist expresses this view; however, the researcher does not evaluate the effect of the system in increasing production.

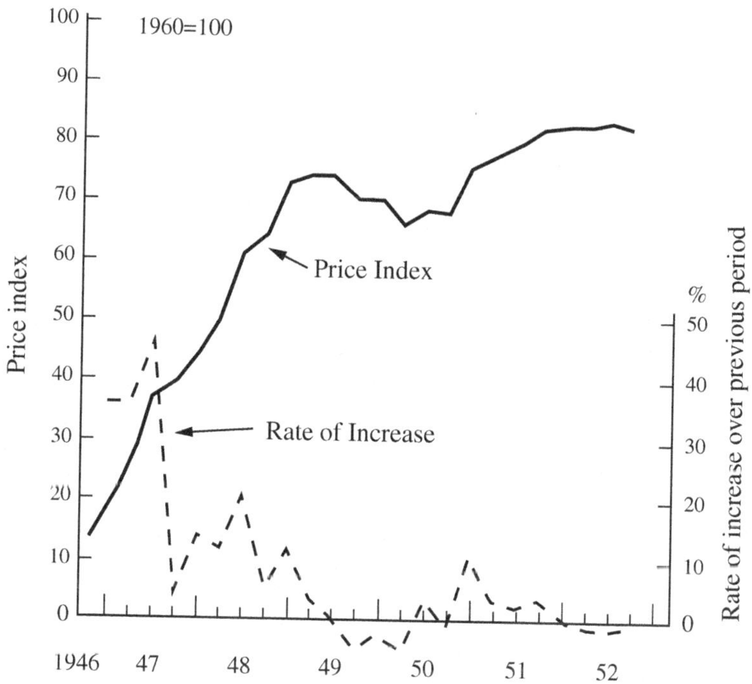

Fig. 2.1 The consumer price index and its rate of increase, 1946–1952. *Note* The index includes black market prices. *Source* Statistics Bureau, Office of the Prime Minister, Nakamura (1981)

As Dr. Shimomura pointed out, the drastic decline in production limited the effect of the Emergency Financial Measures Order and price control order on checking inflation. These measures were temporal. In order to curb inflation, it was essential to increase production. Owing to the Priority Production System, mining and industrial production rapidly increased 26% in 1947 and 32% in 1948, successively. In three years after the war, production recovered to approximately 50% of the prewar peak.

Figure 2.1 shows that the high rate of inflation showed signs of leveling off in early 1948. Particularly, there was a halt in the increase in black market prices. The ratio of black market prices to official prices was 8.3 in 1946, which declined to 5.1 in 1947, and reduced further to 2.9 in 1948. There remains a narrative that Dr. Shimomura, who was in charge of the price control policy of the Economic Stabilization Board (*Keizai Antei Honbu*), walked around the black markets to check the price movement and ascertain whether high rate of inflation was being controlled.[4]

[4]The Economic Stabilization Board was founded in 1946. It exercised economic control over ministries and agencies during the reconstruction period.

2.3 From Reconstruction to High Growth

While inflation continued in the postwar Japanese economy, eventually the government took a policy to increase production and contain inflation. This policy aimed at checking inflation gradually by reviving production. The expansionary policy was in line with Dr. Shimomura's perspective. The government policy focused on realizing equilibrium by expanding economic activity, and this was referred to as the "gradual approach." An idea of expansionary equilibrium later developed into a high growth policy.

Contrarily, there were economists and politicians who prioritized containing inflation. In 1949–1950, very stringent deflationary policy of the Dodge Line was implemented by the Allied Powers, and inflation was abruptly brought under complete control.[5] This policy was referred to as the "single blow stabilization," and was likened to a "shock therapy" that emphasized contractionary equilibrium. The idea of prioritizing the containment of inflation was linked to the stable growth policy of the 1960s.

In 1951, mining and industrial production reached the prewar peak and the Japanese economy finished reconstruction. Around the mid-1950s, trade account became balanced and Japan achieved economic autonomy. A white paper, which analyzed the Japanese economy in 1955, became very famous for the phrase, "we are no longer in the postwar period."

During the reconstruction period from 1946 to 1951, the economic growth rate per annum was as high as 13%. However, during the autonomy period, it dropped to 6% from 1952 to 1954. The mainstream economists expected that the economic growth would naturally decline with the completion of Japanese economic reconstruction. The white paper in 1955 reflected such expectation of experts.

Contrary to the prediction of the white paper and experts, the Japanese economy entered a period of dynamic high growth in the second half of the 1950s. The rate of economic growth did not decelerate, but accelerate.

During the reconstruction period, the aggregate demand exceeded aggregate supply and people suffered from inflation. However, in the mid-1950s, the aggregate supply capacity began to exceed aggregate demand due to a surge in positive investments of private firms in plant and equipment. Dr. Shimomura was the first economist who found this dynamic trend and formulated a new vision and policy of high economic growth.

[5]Dr. Shimomura (1974) commented that inflation could have been contained without the Dodge Line. J. Dodge, a conservative banker in Detroit, came to Japan when inflation began to level off.

2.4 Shimomura Theory

Dr. Shimomura had sharp intuition for grasping complicated economic situations and making economic forecasts. He did not depend on fashionable theories or large-scale econometric computer models. He used his slide rule and had his own economic dynamics, which is referred to as the Shimomura theory. He had completed his theory before the commencement of high economic growth. This enabled him to forecast the approaching era with confidence.

During the immediate postwar period, Dr. Shimomura was in charge of the price control policy in the Ministry of Finance and the Economic Stabilization Board. Owing to the complex nature of the task, he experienced recurrence of lung disease and had to take a long leave to receive medical treatment. He started to write a thesis while he was bedridden. On completion of the work, the full text of the thesis appeared in the monthly research journal of the Ministry of Finance in 1951. In 1952, he published the thesis titled "*Economic Fluctuation and Multiplier Analysis*." He received a doctoral degree for the paper in 1956.

In the preface of the book, Dr. Shimomura (1952) argued that the theory of Keynes was effective to solve actual problems, but that it was also necessary to develop the dynamics of the Keynes theory. Dr. Shimomura wrote as follows.

> When I was a staffer at the Ministry of Finance and later a member of the Commodity Price Agency and the Economic Stabilization Board for several years after the War, the thing that helped me most in tackling my duties in analyzing actual economic trends and prescribing measures to deal with them was the theory of Keynes. At the same time, however, in the process I also became aware of the incompleteness of the theory of Keynes (Shimomura (1952), Economic Fluctuation and Multiplier Analysis).

The main features of the "Economic Fluctuation and Multiplier Analysis" are as follows:

(a) Economic fluctuation is different from economic growth. The former is caused by responsive investment and the latter is realized by autonomous investment.
(b) Profit of a firm fluctuates according to the changes in aggregate demand and aggregate supply. The investment of a firm changes in response to changes in profit. This is called as responsive investment, which causes business cycle in the macro economy. Dr. Shimomura substituted the actual data with parameters of his mathematical model and concluded that a stable investment cycle of approximately 9 years exists in the Japanese economy
(c) Responsive investment changes as the profit changes. Through the feedback system of his model, it realizes stability of the Japanese economy. To conclude, although the capitalist economy fluctuates, it is considered stable.
(d) Autonomous investment of a firm facilitates economic growth, which is not influenced by boom and recession of the economy. An entrepreneurial risk taker carries out investment with a long run perspective. This investment concept is based on Schumpeter's model, which embodies innovation and technological changes. In his model, autonomous investment is expressed as a function of time.

(e) The output-capital ratio estimated by Dr. Shimomura was 1. He used 1935 data from the Cabinet Statistics Bureau and calculated the ratio of national income to industrial asset. In order to consider the potential of high growth in the 1960s, it was very important that output-capital ratio is 1.

Responsive investment leads to a stable business cycle. Dr. Shimomura's model dynamically demonstrated that the capitalist economy was stable. He expressed confidence in the market mechanism. Innovation results in autonomous investment. Dr. Shimomura developed this idea to formulate a high growth theory, and Schumpeter completed the innovation theory to explain business cycles. Dr. Shimomura was the first economist who explicitly used autonomous investment to explain high economic growth.

He developed a dynamic Keynesian theory, following R.F. Harrod and P.A. Samuelson. However, Dr. Shimomura's conclusion was different from Harrod's in that the latter emphasized the instability of the capitalist economy.

Dr. Shimomura's model, referred to as the Shimomura theory, attracted attention. He came to be known among the theoretical academicians. However, he did not seem to be interested in developing his mathematical model further. Instead, he chose a carrier as an economist who worked out solutions to actual issues concerning the economy. He was interested in economic forecasting for entrepreneurs. The Japanese economy entered a stage of high growth in the second half of the 1950s, which was a one-in-a-million event. This historical development seemed to have attracted Dr. Shimomura's attention and interest.

2.5 Concluding Remarks

Dr. Shimomura supported the government policy, which was called as the "gradual approach," to control inflation. This policy aimed to increase industrial production through the Priority Production System and check galloping inflation. The goal of the government was to achieve expansionary equilibrium. In addition, this expansionary policy developed into a high growth policy in the 1960s. Contrarily, other economists and politicians insisted the implementation of a stricter policy to curb demand to control inflation. Referred to as "single blow stabilization," this policy emphasized contractionary equilibrium and was linked to stable growth policy of the 1960s.

Due to lung disease, Dr. Shimomura apparently decided to change his career from a government officer to an economist. He started to write a thesis and completed it in 1951. In his thesis, titled "*Economic Fluctuation and Economic Analysis*," he developed a dynamic Keynesian theory in which he distinguished between business cycle and economic growth.

Dr. Shimomura's mathematical model demonstrated that capitalist economy was stable due to the investment cycle. He clarified that autonomous investment in plant and equipment of a private firm was the main engine of economic growth. He introduced Schumpeter's innovation theory and constructed a growth model. These two aspects constituted the "Shimomura theory" and were essentially important in forming a vision, theory, and policy for high growth in Japan.

The Japanese economy entered a stage of high growth in the second half of the 1950s. He completed and published his economic growth theory to welcome the historical golden age of "Showa." The reconstruction period after the war was a preparatory time for Dr. Shimomura to be active as an economist in the 1960s.

References

Kosai, Y. (1981). *The era of high growth.* Tokyo: Nihon Hyoronsha (in Japanese).

Nakamura, T. (1981). *The postwar Japanese economy.* Tokyo: University of Tokyo Press.

Shimomura, O. (1947). Standard of living in relation to prices. In *Study on the Japanese Economy*. Yodaisha, June/July, 8–16 (in Japanese).

Shimomura, O. (1951). Economic fluctuation and multiplier analysis. *Monthly Research Report*, *40*(3), 61–89; *40*(5), 56–79; *40*(7), 1–86. Ministry of Finance (in Japanese).

Shimomura, O. (1952). *Economic fluctuation and multiplier analysis.* Tokyo: Toyo Keizai Press (in Japanese).

Shimomura, O. (1974). Prices and inflation in the occupation period. In Ministry of Finance (Ed.), *Financial News*, No. 85, March 30. Tokyo: Ministry of Finance (in Japanese).

Chapter 3
Vision of High Growth and Performance in 1960s

Abstract We select nine papers, which Dr. Shimomura published in the 1950s and 1960s, and explain his original vision of high growth, open-macro growth theory, and fiscal and monetary policy for achieving a high growth economy. He is well known as the economic advisor who designed the National Income Doubling Plan for Prime Minister H. Ikeda in 1960. Dr. Shimomura clearly expressed that the Japanese economy would be capable of attaining a growth rate of 10%. His vision that the Japanese economy was witnessing a historical rise encouraged Japan's citizens who were depressed due to the outcome of the war. His long-term forecast of high growth surprised economists, professors, and government officials. He had a famous and heated controversy with them in 1959. Most of them were in favor of stable growth (lower growth). Actually, his forecast turned out to be the most accurate. He proposed a macroeconomic growth policy, which was most proactive and aggressive in the world at that time. The keywords that Dr. Shimomura thought important are innovation, equilibrium, and freedom with self-responsibility. He became a leading economist attracting significant attention from businesspersons.

Keywords High growth · Stable growth · Growth controversy · Innovation · Vision

3.1 Shimomura's Work and His Vision for the Japanese Economy

Dr. Shimomura worked for the Ministry of Finance and was an economic advisor to Prime Minister Ikeda. He became the first director of the Research Institute for Capital Formation of the Japan Development Bank. He subsequently continued to be active in writing and lecturing as an independent economist.

In 1960, Dr. Shimomura was well known as the architect of The National Income Doubling Plan of the Ikeda administration. He published an original theory for the rapid growth of the Japanese economy, wherein he expressed his vision that the Japanese economy saw a historic rise. High economic growth is an epoch-making

K. Horiuchi and M. Otaki, *Dr. Osamu Shimomura's Legacy and the Postwar Japanese Economy*, Development Bank of Japan Research Series,
DOI 10.1007/978-981-10-5762-5_3

and historic event for any nation. He was the leading economist behind high growth policies that were implemented in the 1960s.

In the 1960s, businesspersons paid much attention to economic forecasts, and macroeconomic movements had a strong influence on business activities. There were always two views on economic forecasts; one view was "rapid or high growth," and the other was "stable growth or lower growth." Dr. Shimomura was a leading proponent of high growth, which contributed toward his popularity during the time.

However, he changed his view dramatically during the oil crisis in 1973. At that time, he predicted the "zero economic growth" era. This was an unexpected forecast for the people in Japan. Most economists were critical of his prediction because they thought it was too pessimistic. We will see that the "zero growth" forecast was accurate and it offers a new vision for the twenty first century.

3.1.1 Three Basic Factors for the Foundation of the Vision of High Growth

What are the basic and critical conditions that are necessary for the world economy to grow steadily? In practice, institutions (human-made systems) and natural resources (natural systems) are the two basic factors that are essential for a market economy to work properly. This is especially true when we consider what is necessary for a sustainable world economy in the twenty first century (Table 3.1).

Before the World War II, the world economy was characterized by the following three conditions: the gold standard, block economy (colonialism), and coal. The gold standard and block economy were institutions and coal was natural resources. Owing to these three conditions, growth of the world economy was limited. Economic growth was slow and business cycles often prevailed.

Dr. Shimomura recognized that the post-war world economy was emancipated from the bonds of prewar economic conditions. He expected that the International Monetary Fund (IMF), General Agreement on Tariffs and Trade (GATT), and an abundant supply of low-cost petroleum would facilitate growth in the world economy. These three factors were prerequisite for the steady and healthy economic growth in Japan. The Japanese and world economy could grow simultaneously in the 1960s.

Economists usually point out several economic and social conditions, which they consider characteristics of Japan, and explain the rapid growth of Japan in the 1960s. These are, for example, diligence of workers, a cooperative spirit, preference for savings, high levels of basic education, high quality bureaucrats, among others. In fact, Dr. Shimomura agreed that the Japanese people had these characteristics. However, he believed that there were conditions that can more effectively contribute toward the economic growth of Japan. As per Dr. Shimomura, changes in

Table 3.1 Vison of the Japanese economy

Selected periods	Japanese economy and economic vision	World economy and constraints and growth	General state of economy in Japan
Prewar: –1945	– low-economic growth – business cycle – "Wealthy Nation and Strong Army"	– gold standard system – block economy (colonialism)	– low standard of living – severe unemployment – inflation, deflation
Postwar: 1955–1973	– high economic growth – National Income Doubling Plan – "caching up with advanced economies"	– IMF, GATT, – abundant oil, – simultaneous growth of advanced economies	– full employment – stable prices – growth led by domestic demand – reduction in income differences – expansion in middle class people
After the oil crisis: 1973–2015	– "zero growth" – stationary state – sustainable development	– hike in oil price – limits set by natural resources – constraints of carrying capacity of the earth	– highest standard of living in history – government budget deficit – financial bubble – unstable employment – expansion in income differences

Note Key words of Shimomura theory
Period of high growth: innovation, equilibrium, and freedom with self-responsibility
Period of zero growth: innovation, equilibrium, and discipline
Source Horiuchi (2014)

the post-war economic systems across the globe and energy conditions were essential for ushering growth. He used to say, "The Japanese worked harder before World War II, but they couldn't achieve high economic growth."

In this chapter, we choose nine papers that Dr. Shimomura published in the 1950s and the 1960s and explain how he formulated his vision, theory, and policy for the Japanese economy during the high growth period.

(*Paper 1*)

As we have already mentioned, Dr. Shimomura had confidence in the stability of a capitalist economy due to his original theory of business cycles published in 1951. In this paper ("*Economic Fluctuation and Multiplier Analysis*"), he developed a dynamic Keynesian theory, following R.F. Harrod and P.A. Samuelson. Dr. Shimomura incorporated changes in investment that respond to changes in profit. His model indicated that the Japanese economy had a stable investment cycle of approximately 9 years. In addition, his thesis made a clear distinction between business cycles and economic growth. He pointed out that economic growth is realized through autonomous and high-powered investments, which are carried out by risk-taking and independent entrepreneurs.[1]

In addition to investments, he divided prices into two categories—wholesale prices (prices of manufactured goods) and consumer prices—and defined inflation in a rapidly growing economy. This definition is very useful because inflation in a rapidly growing economy is quite different from inflation experienced during the business cycles of a slow-paced prewar economy. A definition of inflation is very important in terms of making policy decisions, and we will examine it later.

3.1.2 Growth Theory and Long-Term Forecast

Dr. Shimomura focused on creativity and ingenuity of entrepreneurs that had begun to bring forth a rapid increase in autonomous investments in plants and equipment by private firms. He studied statistics on corporate firms closely and found evidence of a surge in such autonomous investments in the latter half of the 1950s. He recognized that rapid increases in investment represented an entrepreneurial spirit and that it was not a temporary phenomenon, but a historical trend. Positive economic policies were necessary to support this dynamic movement. Dr. Shimomura stated clearly that growth policies would psychologically uplift the 94 million people in Japan. His model was a growth version of J.A. Schumpeter's innovation theory.

Schumpeter theorized successfully that innovation caused economic dynamics and business cycles through mechanism of credit creation in the gold standard system. Contrarily, Dr. Shimomura believed that innovation would increase the autonomous investment of a firm and that the supply of growth money through the issuance of government bonds would realize high economic growth. These beliefs of Dr. Shimomura contributed significantly toward the formation of a high growth policy in Japan.

Innovation causes both business cycles and economic growth. In the 1960s, Dr. Shimomura did not focus on business cycles, but he applied innovation theory to economic growth. Autonomous investments undertaken by entrepreneurial risk takers for their firms facilitate economic growth.[2]

Dr. Shimomura's growth theory was formulated in two stages. In the first stage, he estimated the output-capital ratio and found it to be equal to one in the first half of the 1950s; in the second stage, he focused on the rapid increase in investment in the latter half of that decade.

---

[1]Dr. Shimomura's works attracted attention from the academic community, as he presented cutting-edge research at that time [see Uzawa (1991)].

[2]Economists often insist that the reduction of corporate tax will consequently increase the investments of a firm. Investments that are induced by a tax cut are considered weak investments. Autonomous investments are strong investments, which are a function of time. High economic growth is realized by such strong investments.

After his paper was published in 1951, Dr. Shimomura gradually developed the theory of rapid growth and indicated that the Japanese economy witnessed a historic rise.

(*Paper 2*)

In 1955, he published another paper ("*A Tight Monetary Policy; To Understand It Correctly*"), in which he examined empirically the conditions for internal and external equilibrium of the Japanese economy by formulating a savings and investment model in open economy macroeconomics. In this study (1955), we will understand the basic characteristics of Dr. Shimomura's model. First, using data of corporate firms for 1950–1953, he estimated that the output-capital ratio was equal to 1. Second, he took into account and emphasized the condition of macroeconomic equilibrium, which we will discuss later.[3]

Dr. Shimomura did not write anything about how fast the Japanese economy would grow, but he suggested a possibility that the Japanese economy would face an excess of aggregate supply relative to aggregate demand. In a growing economy, new investment increases production capacity and demand. He estimated that an increase in production capacity might be greater than an increase in aggregate demand. The Japanese economy would be in a state of overproduction. In conclusion, he wrote, "*Unless the government increases its public expenditure sufficiently, investment of a firm would be in a deadlock.*" In order to avoid this difficulty, it was necessary to undertake positive public investment expansion. Dr. Shimomura gradually developed this idea, which was embodied in the National Income Doubling Plan.[4]

[3]According to Murakami (1971), Dr. Shimomura's paper was a painstaking and pioneering work in a sense that he was the first economist who applied the macroeconomic theory after Keynes to the real Japanese economy. Murakami added that this paper was a classic, which should be remembered.

[4]His model (1955) is as follows.

(a) Internal equilibrium

Increase in supply: $\Delta YS = \sigma I_{-1}$
Increase in demand: $\Delta YD = \{1/(s + t + m)\}(\Delta I + \Delta G + \Delta X)$
Supply − demand: $\Delta YS - \Delta YD = \Delta Y$

(b) External equilibrium

An increase in export = an increase in import: $\Delta X = \Delta M = m\Delta Y$
Values of parameters: $\sigma = 1.0$, $s = 0.3$, $t = 0.27$, $m = 0.13$;
then $\Delta I + \Delta G = 4.4\Delta X$
$I_{-1} = 7.7\Delta X$

Where, ΔYS is an increase in supply, σ is output-capital ratio, I_{-1} is investment in previous year, ΔYD denotes an increase in demand, ΔI stands for an increase in industrial investment, ΔG stands for an increase in public expenditure, ΔX denotes an increase in export, ΔM represents an increase in import, s is saving ratio, t stands for tax rate, and m stands for import ratio.

(*Paper 3*)

In 1958, Dr. Shimomura published a paper ("*Realizing Economic Growth*") wherein he mentioned that the Japanese economy was at an important turning point, having transitioned from an economy characterized by an excess of demand to that of an excess of supply. During the reconstruction period, after the World War II, the Japanese economy suffered from inflation due to an excess demand over supply. Dr. Shimomura recognized that this situation was ending. Furthermore, he expressed clearly the need for a positive fiscal and monetary policy to stimulate economic growth. In the aforementioned study, he suggested the possibility of achieving a growth rate of 10%. This study offered a theoretical foundation for the National Income Doubling Plan launched in 1960.

The maximum rate of economic growth was limited by the two following factors: reserve forces in domestic supply capacity and imports. In the paper (1958), he verified that investments in Japan increased annually to more than about 1 trillion yen, which meant that an annual increase in real GNP of about 1 trillion yen could have been possible without the international balance of payment being in red. This implied that the Japanese economy had a potential to grow at a rate of 10% annually. Dr. Shimomura, a proponent of high growth policy, criticized the so-called "stable growth" policy that targeted lower growth. As per Dr. Shimomura, economic growth is realized through the innovation of free and private entrepreneurs.

Shimomura (1958) wrote as follows.

> Japan's economy is now at an important turning point. Over the years since the end of the War, our efforts had been directed to how we could suppress aggregate demand, which tended to exceed the aggregate supply capacity. Now, however, we have reached the point where we should discuss how to utilize our improved supply capabilities to realize sound economic growth.
>
> We should welcome this change in circumstances as a sign of Japan's robust economic growth potential. Yet, even now economic growth continues to be unnecessarily constrained, and there is a tendency to purposefully ignore the undesirable effects of holding the economy back. This is due to a failure of policymakers to recognize this fundamental change in the Japanese economy. This is an approach we cannot support.
>
> It is now time for the government to make active efforts to realize economic growth and development through comprehensive and flexible use of fiscal and monetary policies. … Our basic position is that the direction of aggregate effective demand adjustments must be changed from a negative policy of dampening excess demand to a positive policy of realizing growth potential.
>
> Our aim is to realize the highest possible economic growth, as quickly and as stably as possible. This does not mean that there should be a specific target rate for economic growth. We respect the principle that economic growth has to be the product of the creative activities, daring and self-responsibility of entrepreneurs…. Thus, aiming to attain a specific growth rate, while artificially restricting entrepreneurial activities, is neither realistic, nor is it a basis on which to sustain vigorous economic growth.
>
> [Shimomura (1958), "Realizing Economic Growth"]

(*Paper 4*)

In 1959, Shimomura published a paper ("*The Fundamentals of the Japanese Economy and its Growth Potential—A critique of the excessive growth thesis and an examination of Japan's growth potential*"). In this paper (1959a), he expressed clearly that the Japanese economy would be capable of attaining a 10% per annum rate of growth; he also pointed out that the economy witnessed a historic rise. He revealed that the expected rate of growth of 6.5% per annum in the New Long-Term Economic Plan of the government (1958–1962) would be too low. On the contrary, at that time, professors and economists considered 6.5% to be a very high rate and hence were critical of the expectations. Therefore, the 10% growth theory of Dr. Shimomura was not well accepted in the professional academic circle and triggered the famous "growth controversy."[5] Dr. Shimomura (1959a) wrote as follows.

> Expressed in broad terms, the conclusion is that the Japanese economy at present has the potential to lift its GNP by around one trillion yen each year. If annual investment reaches roughly 1.5 trillion yen, the supply capacity is expected to rise enough to enable an increase in GNP several hundred billions more than one trillion yen per annum. And an annual increase in exports of 250 million dollars each year would be sufficient to cover the additional imports generated by an annual GNP increase of one trillion yen.
>
> A GNP increase of one trillion yen per annum would translate to a growth rate of approximately 10% under the present conditions. This is far larger than the 6.5% growth predicted in the Five-Year Plan (the New Long-Term Economic Plan). Given that even the economic growth rate predicted in the Five-Year Plan is considered to be too high, our claim may appear extraordinary. Nevertheless, although it has gone unnoticed, Japan's economy has already reached the stage where such a high level of GNP growth is now attainable.
>
> [Shimomura (1959a), "The Fundamentals of the Japanese Economy and its Growth Potential"]

3.1.3 *Growth Controversy in 1959*

Dr. Shimomura (1959a) surprised policymakers and economists. They were S. Okita, S. Tsuru, T. Yoshino, among others. They found it difficult to comprehend Dr. Shimomura's view of 10% growth. The high economic growth theory was regarded a kind of heterodoxy, however, the controversy did not hinder Dr. Shimomura's discussions on the subject with mainstream people. It was believed that, post—the reconstruction period, the Japanese economy would experience decelerating growth, and that the excess capital investments would lead to overproduction. This was contrary to the view expressed in Dr. Shimomura's positive theory.

---

[5]See Shimomura (1971) for his collected papers.

The most important parameter of Dr. Shimomura's theory was the aggregate output-capital ratio, which he estimated at 1. This means that investments in capital stock of this year would realize the same amount of increase in aggregate supply capacity in terms of GNP next year. Moreover, in his theory, the capital stock consisted of investments of private firms and did not include public investments. This is different from common theory in which the capital stock consists of private and public investments. Dr. Shimomura believed that productive capacity of a country is based on capital stock of a private sector. Public capital stock would be constructed in the course of economic growth. These two conditions and his assumptions about other parameters, such as the import ratio, caused intense debate. This debate took place in 1959 and was referred to as the "growth controversy."[6]

Leading professors and economists in the government and banks participated in the controversy. They discussed the definition of economic variables, such as output-capital ratio, and published their own estimates of the parameters. S. Okita, who was responsible for the New Long Term Economic Plan of the government, criticized Dr. Shimomura on the following matters. First, he believed that Dr. Shimomura's estimate of output-capital ratio was high because the Japanese economy finished postwar reconstruction. Second, Dr. Shimomura was criticized for considering the import ratio of 9.5% as slightly low. Third, the European economy was expected to grow slowly, and a slowdown was projected for the world trade. These factors were expected to result in slower export growth in Japan, thereby affecting the Japanese economic growth. Most economists agreed with Okita and held the upward inflection of growth rate that Dr. Shimomura proclaimed as baseless. However, Okita approved that a positive policy, which Dr. Shimomura insisted, was necessary and expressed that he agreed with Dr. Shimomura in many respects.

T. Yoshino, an economist at the Bank of Japan, was Dr. Shimomura's opponent in an argument and was a famous proponent of stable economic growth theory. Yoshino considered stability in economic growth to be very important; he emphasized on economic growth that is associated with lower levels of inflation and less economic fluctuations. According to Yoshino, economic policy should be neither positive nor aggressive, but be moderate to a certain extent and focus on economic development that is steady despite smaller disturbances. Stable growth implies lower growth. Although he did not mention any figure or estimate on growth rate, it must have been much lower than Dr. Shimomura's estimate of 10%.

[6]In many cases, capital includes public and private investments. This was one of the most important points in the controversy. Dr. Shimomura insisted that the investment of private firms forms the basis for the productive capacity of a country. He believed that rapid growth would make it possible for the government to allocate resources to invest in public infrastructure. According to the capital stock data, the output-capital ratio for Japan was 1.1 in the 1960s and 0.5 in the 1970s. It declined further due to an increase in investments for pollution control and energy-saving [see Horiuchi (1998)].

Yoshino had his own theory that high growth would cause problems such as overproduction, deficit of the balance of payment, and hike in consumer price.[7]

Some scholars, such as S. Tsuru, expressed pessimistic views on the economic growth possibilities of Japan as a capitalist economy. They raised questions about Dr. Shimomura's vision of the Japanese economy.[8]

The discussion focused on technical details such as the output-capital ratio and import ratio. Economists did not consider Shimomura's vision that the Japanese economy was on a historic rise.

This controversy was in the form of the most serious and intense economic debate in the post-war period. At that time, the Japanese economy underwent postwar reconstruction and stood at the crossroads where one road led to a high growth path and the other to a low growth path. Unlike the prevailing view at the time, Dr. Shimomura expressed a clear opinion that the Japanese economy would experience accelerated growth in the 1960s.

(*Paper 5*)

Dr. Shimomura took into account the issues and questions raised during the "growth controversy" in 1959. During the meeting of the Theoretical Economic Society in Japan in 1960, he announced the long-term economic projections (up to 1970) (Shimomura (1961a), ("*Basic Issues on Growth Policy*"). This forecast was called the Shimomura Plan[9]. He showed that 10.6% growth per annum would be possible under the conditions of price stability, a balanced government budget, and international trade current account balance[10].

---

[7]Dr. Shimomura and R. Komiya were critical proponents of a stable growth theory because their way of thinking was occupied with experience acquired during the prewar gold standard days [see Nakayama and Economist (1960)].

[8]Papers of Dr. Shimomura, Okita, Yoshino, Tsuru, and other economists, who participated in "growth controversy," were compiled in the Kinzai Institute for Financial Affairs (Ed.) (1959).

[9]As per Dr. Shimomura's Plan, the net investment (In) was used for output-capital ratio ($\sigma = 1$). The ratio of replacement investment to gross investment was estimated to increase from 15% in 1961 to 20% in 1970. An increase in aggregate supply capacity (ΔYc) was calculated as $\Delta Yc = \sigma \bullet In_{-1} = In_{-1}$

[10]The essence of dynamism of high growth economy will be summarized as follows,

1. Aggregate investment of previous year (I_{-1}) increases the same amount of aggregate supply capacity of this year (ΔYc), whereas an increase in aggregate investment (ΔI) increases aggregate demand (ΔYd) by multiplier effect.

   $\Delta Yc = \sigma \bullet I_{-1}$, where σ is output-capital ratio and 1.
   $\Delta Yd = 1/s \bullet \Delta I$
   As σ is large, an increase in aggregate supply capacity (ΔYc) exceeds an increase in the aggregate demand (ΔYd).
   $\Delta Yc > \Delta Yd$

2. As autonomous investment increases rapidly, aggregate investment (I) exceeds aggregate savings (S), which pushes up the aggregate effective demand.

   $I > S$.

It is reported that most economists that attended the aforementioned meeting in 1960 were critical of the long-term prediction made by Dr. Shimomura. Although they examined the intricacies, they failed to understand the bigger-picture communicated through Dr. Shimomura's vision. It must be understood that the annual growth rate of 10% projected by Dr. Shimomura exceeded the 7.2% growth rate that was set in the National Income Doubling Plan of the government.

In 1960, only a few people supported Dr. Shimomura's long-term forecast. However, it turned out that his forecast was very close to the actual growth rate of the economy of 10.4% per annum. His forecast made the people of Japan confident that their country can achieve a high growth rate.

The macroeconomic policies proposed by Dr. Shimomura were considered some of the most proactive policies in the world at that time. He clearly stated that large tax cuts and massive increases in government expenditure were necessary to fill the shortage of aggregate demand relative to the rapidly increasing aggregate supply capacity. As a result, the Japanese economy was successfully put on the track of warranted growth in Harrod's sense.

Dr. Shimomura's growth policy was more positive and aggressive than the growth policies in the US and Europe. Dr. Shimomura had a clear vision of the Japanese economy, which we will discuss in the next section. Therefore, he had a confidence in his long-run forecast.

According to his estimate, the output-capital ratio was equal to 1; in addition, he expected private investments to register a continual and rapid increase. These factors led to a rapid increase in the aggregate supply capacity. He insisted that the government's role was to assist the private sector in realizing its potential ability by using positive fiscal and monetary policies. He often said that the government was only a supporting actor and diligent people played the major role.

Dr. Shimomura placed high value on the ability and vitality of the private sector. Generally, his view on this matter was different from that of the bureaucrats in Japan. The people in Japan held government's viewpoint in high regard, instead of the private sector; this tendency was evident in the pre-war days and it continued even in the postwar era.

3.1.4 New Vision of the Japanese Economy in 1961–1962

At the end of the 1950s, Dr. Shimomura announced his 10% growth forecast. At the same time, he presented his historical view of the Japanese and world economy, which we refer to as Dr. Shimomura's vision. He expressed this vision during a phase when the Japanese economy was witnessing a historic development or surge. He pointed out that a majority of people in Japan, including the intellectuals, were unaware of the scenario at that time.

As described previously, before World War II, the world economy was characterized by three conditions: the gold standard, block economies (colonialism) and expensive coal. Owing to these three conditions, growth of the world economy was limited. Economic growth was slow and business cycles often prevailed. However, Dr. Shimomura recognized that the world economy post-World War II was emancipated from the bonds of prewar economic conditions. He expected the IMF, GATT, and an abundant supply of low-cost petroleum to facilitate growth in the world economy.

The immediate post-war world economy was characterized by the setting up of the IMF and GATT. While the IMF aimed at achieving full employment and higher living standards on an international scale, the free trade principles of GATT aimed at contributing toward the upgradation of Japan's industrial structure. In addition, we should note that the US economy was sound and balanced.

These three factors were prerequisite to the steady and healthy growth of the Japanese economy. The Japanese economy and the world economy could have grown simultaneously in the 1960s.

(*Paper 6*)

In 1959, Shimomura wrote several papers to express his vision. Shimomura's (1959b) "*Growth Theory and the Growth Potential of the Japanese Economy*" was one of them.

In this paper, Dr. Shimomura compares the growth rate and the level and share of investment in GNP of major economies, and statistically demonstrates how Japan's performance stands out. He states that, "*the government can effectively adjust aggregate effective demand through fiscal or monetary policy, and that it is its responsibility to do so in a reasonable manner.*"

He also emphasizes the need for active expansionary policies to make full use of the increase in supply capacity.

> As stated above, it is clear that Japan's economy is now undergoing an historic episode in its development or a sudden rise in its prosperity. Some might question why is it that Japan's growth potential shows no sign of declining, even though the postwar reconstruction period is over? Yet those who see Japan's continued high growth as abnormal are overlooking the fundamental conditions that determine the economic growth.
>
> [Shimomura (1959b), "Growth Theory and the Growth Potential of the Japanese Economy"]

(*Paper 7*)

Economic growth is realized through the historical and daily life of people. It is an expression of "spiritual awakening" in the whole nation. In his paper, "*The Current Economic Conditions and How to Deal With Them*", Dr. Shimomura (1961b) gives an account of the prospects of the Japanese economy, which was in a process of historical transformation. As rapid growth was being realized, He expressed his views clearly and strongly. Dr. Shimomura (1961b) wrote as follows.

> Today, spiritual awakening and innovation are taking root all over Japan. Undoubtedly, this will eventually manifest itself as a substantial leap in the creative powers of 94 million people. Through the robust, rationalization and modernization of investment, the Japanese people are demonstrating their ability to steer this turbulent process in a realistic and rational direction. This is the reality of the current phase of Japan's economic growth. This

growth mentality should not be regarded as frivolous. Rather it must be regarded as an expression of a spiritual awakening that distinguishes a new historical period of vigorous ascent.

[Shimomura (1961b), "The Current Economic Conditions and How to Deal With Them"]

(*Paper 8*)

Dr. Shimomura (1962) expressed his own views on economy and history. A notable point was that he was not interested in planned economy. There may be three reasons for it. First, owing to his prewar experience in controlling prices as a government officer, he recognized that state control was inefficient. Second, based on his doctoral thesis that was published in 1951, he showed that the Japan was a stable capitalist country. Third, factors to induce investment were not necessarily clear in Marxian economics. In addition, the National Income Doubling Plan of 1960 differs from economic plans of the socialist countries.

His economic vision and growth forecast encouraged the people of Japan, who lost confidence in postwar Japanese economy. Dr. Shimomura (1962) in his "*A Theory of Japanese Economic Growth*" offered a compelling account in the following words.

Productivity is the foundation of the economy, and it is the people's creativity that propels its development. … I am not an advocate of planned economic growth. … My interest lies not in planning, but in the pursuit of possibilities. I am interested not in controlling people's activities to match a blueprint someone else has prepared, but in examining the conditions that are necessary for development and liberation of the people's creativity. … Liberated from the shackles of colonialism and the gold standard, today's world economy is about to enter a new era. … This gives us hope and confidence. For the first time ever, we are poised to experience an historic modernization of agriculture and small- and medium-sized enterprises. We could not have hoped for this in the prewar period. This new current in world history is now supporting a historic rise in the Japanese economy.

[Shimomura (1962), "A Theory of Japanese Economic Growth"]

Dr. Shimomura's economic policy was developed based on the standpoint of "Economy for the people." He provided a new historical perspective after the war and encouraged the people of Japan to change their mindset. In this sense, his vision of high growth was more than an ordinary economic forecast; in fact, it went beyond standard economics.

3.2 Performance of the 1960s (1960–1970, 11 Years)

During this period, the Japanese economy attained high growth. The important question is whether the realized growth was stable. At that time, the economists emphasized two equilibrium conditions for achieving stable growth: internal equilibrium and external equilibrium. These conditions were discussed continuously in policy debates during the 1960s.

Table 3.2 Long term trends of the Japanese economy (Annual average, %)

Calendar year	1955–1959	1960–1970	1971–1982	1983–1985	1986–1990	1991–1995
GDP (real-term)	8.0	10.4	4.2	3.5	4.6	1.4
Private						
Consumption	7.9	9.2	4.4	3.1	4.4	1.9
Housing investment	10.1	17.6	2.0	−1.9	9.3	2.3
Firm's investment	16.6	18.4	2.6	8.4	10.0	−2.4
Public						
Consumption	3.0	4.8	4.6	1.7	2.5	2.4
Investment	8.1	14.2	4.6	−4.1	3.7	7.5
External						
Exports	12.2	15.6	8.9	8.2	3.0	4.3
Imports	10.7	15.2	4.3	1.8	11.6	3.6
Price increase						
Wholesale price	−0.1	1.3	6.5	−1.2	−2.0	−1.6
Consumer price	0.6	5.6	8.1	2.0	1.4	1.4
Balance of payment/GDP						
Trade account	0.0	1.0	1.6	3.4	3.3	3.1
Current account	0.1	0.1	0.6	2.7	2.8	2.6

Note Classification of periods is as follows
1955–1970: high growth (1955–1959: early period, 1960–1970: full-scale)
1971–1982: export-oriented and low growth since 1973, start of "zero growth"
1983–1985: Reagan Shock (appreciation of dollar, rapid export increase to the US)
1986–1990: bubble economy (appreciation of yen, expansion of domestic demand)
1991–1995: zero growth (bubble burst, appreciation of yen)
Source Economic planning agency "Annual Statistics on National Economy", Bank of Japan "Annual Report on Economic Statistics", Horiuchi (2007)

3.2.1 *Rate of Growth of the Japanese Economy*

Economic growth in terms of real GDP from 1960 to 1970 was 10.4% per annum, which was almost equal to what Dr. Shimomura expected in 1960. The main engine for this rapid growth was private investment by firms that surged to 18.4% per annum in real terms (see Table 3.2).

3.2.2 *Internal Equilibrium*

Internal equilibrium means two things: stable prices and a balanced government budget. There are two kinds of prices, wholesale prices (prices of manufactured goods) and consumer prices. This distinction is important to understand inflation in a rapidly growing economy.

1. Stable wholesale prices

In a rapidly growing economy that is characterized by rapidly increasing labor productivity in the manufacturing sector, price stability refers to stable prices of manufactured goods (wholesale prices). In Japan, manufactured goods are the main tradable commodities. During the 1960s, the stability of wholesale prices led to a stable foreign exchange rate in the IMF system. The economy does not experience high inflation as long as wholesale prices remain stable. Stable wholesale prices form the basis for maintaining constant purchasing power parity and a fixed exchange rate in the IMF system.

Wholesale prices remained stable and increased only 1.3% per annum during the period of 10% growth. This was mainly realized because the average annual rate of increase in labor productivity (11.4%) was almost equal to that of the wages (11.9%) in manufacturing industries. The efforts of working people were rewarded properly due to the maintenance of a fixed exchange rate. In this manner, Dr. Shimomura provided a clear definition of price stability. However, this point was not fully recognized by policymakers, which caused the "price controversy." The government became too cautious about a rise in consumer prices. This led to several flaws in the formation of economic policy. Consumer prices began to rise suddenly as the economy achieved full employment around 1961. In 1964, the trade balance fell into deficit. Against this backdrop, a restrictive monetary policy was implemented in 1964 and the Japanese economy fell into recession in 1965.

(*Paper 9*)

Dr. Shimomura was very critical of the restrictive policy, which was hailed by economists in favor of stable economic growth. Dr. Shimomura (1965) wrote the following about the essence of price stability in his paper "*The advocates of stable growth defeated!*"

> To strengthen the incentives for innovation for those who are engaged in economic activity, it is extremely important to prepare the conditions for an increase in income in line with the rise in productivity. It is only natural that people's efforts to increase productivity are maximized when they are guaranteed adequate remuneration for being efficient. This is the biggest factor in stimulating economic growth. …
>
> There is a relationship between the large potential inherent in the Japanese economy today, a stable foreign exchange rate and stable wholesale prices. I believe this relationship supports, to the maximum extent possible, those forces that stimulate technological innovation and productivity improvement.
>
> In any case, wholesale price stability is the most important aim of economic and monetary policy. Maintaining stable wholesale prices fosters economic growth and increases people's incomes. At the same time, given that during the economic growth process increases in consumer prices vary from country to country, it would only cause unnecessary confusion to target consumer price stability directly.
>
> [Shimomura (1965), "The advocates of stable growth defeated!"]

2. Increase in consumer prices

Consumer prices in Japan increased by 5.6% per annum from 1960 to 1970. Many economists thought that this rate was very high. An economist at the Bank of Japan sometimes insisted that the Japanese economy was inflationary and expressed an opinion that the government should use restrictive policy.

Dr. Shimomura dismissed this argument as being obsessed with a theory of the prewar gold standard days. In the prewar period, the economy grew very slowly and business cycles were dominant. Prices surged during the boom period and declined during recession. Dr. Shimomura believed that in a growing economy, under a managed currency system, wholesale prices would remain stable and consumer prices would increase at a constant rate, and thus an increase in consumer prices in a growing economy is normal and healthy. According to him, inflation meant a hike in wholesale prices.

Consumer prices consist of two prices, the prices of manufactured goods (wholesale prices) and the charges/rates of service industries. The productivity of service industries tends to increase very slowly as compared to that of the manufacturing industries. However, there was a rapid rise in overall wages when the Japanese economy reached the stage of full employment. The average rate of unemployment was 1.3% in the 1960s. These facts led to an increase in the charges of service industries, and consumer prices started to go up at a faster pace during the period. An increase in consumer prices is a natural consequence of economic growth under full employment, that is, an increase in the value of labor relative to the value of commodities. It implies that human value increases faster than the value of goods.[11]

Therefore, Dr. Shimomura argued that the rate of increase of consumer price depends on the rate of economic growth; rapid economic growth leads to a higher increase in consumer prices. The rate of increase of consumer price depends on economic growth rate and hence cannot become the target of government economic policy [see Dr. Shimomura's paper (1965)].

The economy faced a labor shortage in the 1960s consequently leading to a rapid increase in the wages of low-income workers. The wage differentials reduced between the high-income and low-income laborers, thereby improving income inequality. As a result, a majority of people in Japan started considering themselves a part of the middle class strata. High growth improved the living standard of people who had been economically disadvantaged.

[11]The general tendency in Japan at the time was as follows. In calculating consumer prices, the weight of manufactured goods was 0.5 and that of services was 0.5. The economy grew 10% annually. In manufacturing industries, the increase in productivity and wages were 10% annually. In service industries, the increase in productivity was 0 and wages increased 10% annually, under full employment. Subsequently, the wholesale prices remained stable and consumer prices increased 5% annually.

3. Principle of balanced government budget

The government cut tax rates in the 1960s, but tax revenue was increasing very rapidly. Tax revenue was enough to meet the current expenditure, including interest payments on government bonds. If the government had not cut taxes, the fiscal balance would have recorded a large surplus.

Tax cuts stimulate the economy and this was the case in Japan. However, generally, tax cuts do not lead to a balanced budget, unless the response of the private sector is strong. In a rapidly growing economy, there is a relatively large response to a tax cut. Moreover, it is important to note that such economy leads to a sharp surge in autonomous investment. Although the government cuts taxes, government budget is kept balanced. This was true for the Japanese economy in the 1960s. In a different situation, the tax cut policy would have resulted in a government budget deficit as was experienced during the Reagan administration in the US in the 1980s.

The expenditure for public investment was financed by issuing government bonds. This system is referred to as the "principle of construction bonds." This principle prohibited the government from issuing deficit-covering bonds, which finance current expenditure. In case of issuing these bonds, special law must be approved by the Diet. The issuance of government bonds from the mid-1960s did not cause crowding-out in the capital market.

At the beginning of the 1960s, the firm's demand for money was very strong, but there was not enough liquidity in the financial market. The interest rates were very high compared to the corporate earnings rate. A firm faced difficulty in borrowing funds necessary for investment. In 1963, Dr. Shimomura wrote a paper "*Financial Normalization and Low Interest Rates Revolution,*" wherein he criticized the government policy. He insisted that the government should issue bonds and the Bank of Japan should buy them through open market operation. Dr. Shimomura insisted strongly that financial market should be normalized and the interest rate should be lowered. In 1965, the government started to issue bonds, and a money supply system that is necessary for economic growth was established gradually.

3.2.3 External Equilibrium

External equilibrium means that the international balance of payments should be in equilibrium in the long run. The ratio of current account surplus to nominal GDP in Japan was 0.1% on average during 1960–1970 (see Table 3.2). During this period, external equilibrium was achieved in Japan.

During this period, the rate of increase in exports (in real terms) was 15.6% per annum and the rate of increase in imports (in real terms) was 15.2% per annum. Exports and imports rose at nearly the same pace, and there was no surplus or deficit in the international balance of payments. Therefore, the rapid growth in Japan in the 1960s can be referred to as domestic demand-induced growth and not export-oriented growth. An increase in exports stimulated domestic demand, particulary, investment by firms. However, domestic demand was independently increasing very rapidly, which brought about an increase in imports. An increase in exports was necessary to finance the growth in imports. In addition, the world economy was expanding rapidly, which enabled Japanese exports to grow rapidly. Exports were just enough to equal imports.[12]

It is often pointed out that Japan grew successfully because of export-oriented growth. However, in reality, Japanese growth was realized by an increase in domestic demand. This growth pattern of Japan was opposite to that in China and Asian countries, which are export–oriented.

3.2.4 Industrial Policy

The finding in the previous section reflects the industrial policy of the government to foster infant industries. These industries were expected to grow and become competitive in the world market. Japan is a country with a large population, and it should accommodate a variety of industries—from materials and parts industries to process and assembly industries—to maintain full employment. This was referred to as the "one set principle." This principle was a typical example of industrial policy, which was consistent with domestic demand-induced growth.

Contrarily, governments of countries with a small population usually formulate industrial policies that support free trade to attain export-oriented growth. Generally, a few specialized industries that are efficient and globally competitive are present in countries with a small population.

We will see in Fig. 3.1 that the relationship between population size and import ratio (import/GDP) of a country is negative. The more populated a country is, the lesser is its import ratio. A populous country has a variety of industries domestically and a low import ratio. A surge in the import ratio of a populous country may be a sign of industrial hollowing. This tendency has appeared clearly in the US economy. The import ratio of the US increased from 3.1% in 1965 to 8.5% in 1985. The issue of industrial hollowing will be discussed in chapter 5.

The heavy and chemical industry policy of the 1950s and early 1960s probably most accurately typifies Japan's industrial policy. The Ministry of International Trade and Industry (MITI) chose key industries and formulated concrete strategies to protect and foster these industries during their infancy. Industrial development, particularly the development of manufacturing industry, was extremely important for Japan's economic growth.

The protectionist industry-fostering policies or import substitution policies were successful. However, at the end of 1950s, these policies underwent a gradual

[12]After the oil crisis, however, exports increased and domestic demand remained weak; as a result, the Japanese economy became export-oriented.

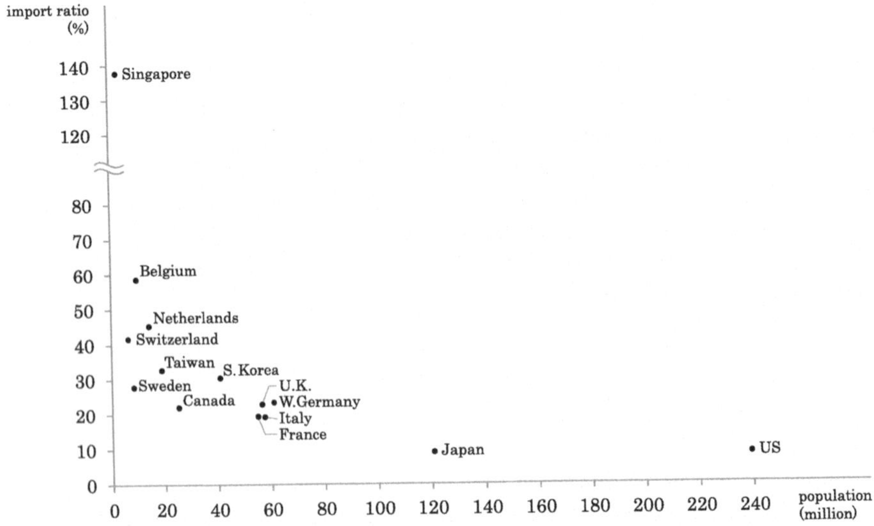

Fig. 3.1 Population size and import ratio (1985). *Note* Import ratio = commodity import/nominal GDP. *Source*: IMF "International Financial statistics"

change. Trade liberalization was promoted as a means to raise effectively industrial efficiency and value-added productivity. If people seize potential future challenges and look ahead with enthusiasm, as was the case in Japan during the high growth period, then the growth policies based on gradual liberalization will prove successful.

Japan's industrial policies emphasized efficiency and market results. Owing to this, corporations in Japan were able to grow their line of business and concentrated on their core product and industrial ideals. Competition for expanded market share, which is a characteristic of Japanese companies, brought about the realization of economies of scale through active investments in plant and equipment.

3.3 Concluding Remarks

Dr. Shimomura played an important role as an economist and contributed toward the high growth in Japan. Hedberg (1969), a Swedish journalist, wrote that Dr. Shimomura was a strong candidate for Nobel Prize of Economics in the 1970s. According to Professor Uzawa, Dr. Shimomura used a simple number to express the core of economic analysis. As a typical example, the output-capital ratio of the Japanese economy was 1, the annual rate of economic growth was 10% in the 1960s and "zero" % after 1973.

Furthermore, Uzawa pointed out that Dr. Shimomura had a great intuition for macro economy, which was demonstrated in the famous growth controversy that occurred in 1959. Although the high economic growth theory was regarded heterodoxy, he continued discussing on the subject with mainstream people. These people supported the forecasts on slower growth. Dr. Shimomura criticized the theorists of stable growth because they were occupied with experiences obtained during the prewar gold standard days.

Dr. Shimomura was different from other economists. He had a clear vision of high growth. Vision, theory, and data analysis are three important factors that enable an economist to propose an economic policy. Economists that propagated stable growth lacked a clear vision and proposed a wrong policy, which caused the recession in 1965. This principle is true today. A growth-oriented policy in case of a zero-growth world economy causes large deficits in the government budget, thereby increasing the supply of money by a central bank. Dr. Shimomura showed us that a clear vision is very important to formulate an economic policy.

High growth is not something that can be realized by simply applying economic theory to the real world. It is considered a historic event that involves an entire nation as a whole in which majority of people expect and believe that high growth would be possible. Dr. Shimomura's insight recognized the emerging willingness of the Japanese people to lead better lives at the beginning of the 1960s. This was the basis of his clear vision of high growth. In addition, his vision encouraged the Japanese people to realize historic rise of the Japanese economy.

Let us summarize the main characteristics of the Japanese economy in the 1960s. The rapid growth in Japan facilitated the internal and external equilibrium conditions, and hence the economy in the 1960s can be considered stable.

The vision of Dr. Shimomura's high growth economy contributed to a change in the consciousness and thinking of Japanese people when they lost confidence after the war. The rapid growth developed a sense of certainty for the future in the minds of people. Long-term forecasts based on a correct vision were extremely important and inspired Japanese people to believe in a new paradigm for the future of their country.

Managing fiscal and monetary policies to achieve the internal and external balance simultaneously is fundamental for achieving stability in economic growth. Under this kind of disciplined economic management, a nation and its people can realize their maximum potential effectively. The Japanese economy in the 1960s had attained expansionary equilibrium, owing to the establishment of the IMF and GATT and availability of oil at lower prices. In addition, high economic growth in excess of 10% per annum was achieved while maintaining both fiscal and current account balance. This high growth was brought about by private sector investments in plant and equipment.

During the 1960s, private sector investments showed an annual increase of 18.4%. Positive tax reduction policies and expanded public investment stimulated private sector investments. At the same time, autonomous investments were increasing rapidly. An increase in autonomous investments together with increase in investments induced by tax cuts facilitated high economic growth, which yielded a substantial increase in tax revenues. Despite active fiscal policies, tax reduction resulted in equilibrium between fiscal revenues and expenditures.

Equilibrium was also maintained in the current accounts in the balance of payments. This showed that the high growth in the 1960s was domestic demand-induced growth and not export-oriented growth. This result was consistent with industrial policy for a populous country like Japan.

At that time, another characteristic of the Japanese economy was the stable relationship between productivity and wages that contributed toward stability in wholesale prices (prices of manufactured goods) over a long period. Stability of wholesale prices is a prerequisite for a stable economic growth and foreign exchange rate. Government policies actively increased effective demand; additionally, prices, including exchange rates, were stable. Under these favorable conditions, a firm acts more boldly, and entrepreneurs display greater ingenuity. The animal spirits mentioned by Keynes is the most important factor that contributes to a firm's decision to proceed with long-term investments. Investment made now is influenced by what a firm expects about future prospects.

The rapid economic growth reduced income inequality and led a majority of people to consider that they belonged to the middle class.

The active economic policies in Japan successfully enabled the private sector to undertake bold initiatives. Both the government and private enterprise pursued high growth, which, in turn, brought about economic stability. Overall, high growth in the 1960s was realized under domestic equilibrium (including stable manufactured goods prices and fiscal balance) and an external equilibrium (balanced current account).

In the 1960s, the government and private sector had a common goal. People worked very hard, collaborated toward economic growth and mutually witnessed economic success. This period was referred to as the "good old Showa" era.

We reviewed Dr. Shimomura's vision, theory and policy, and economic history in the 1960s. The high growth achieved during this period can be attributed to the following factors: innovation, equilibrium, and freedom with self-responsibility.

References

Hedberg, H. H. (1969). *The Japanese challenge*. Stockholm: Bonniers.

Horiuchi, K. (1998). *Vision and policy of the Japanese economy: From growth to development*. Tokyo: Toyo Keizai Press (in Japanese).

Horiuchi, K. (2007). *Dr. Shimomura and the Japanese economy*. Tokyo: Development Bank of Japan, Research Institute of Capital Formation (in Japanese).

Horiuchi, K. (2014). Vision of the Japanese economy and social common capital. In Y. Mamiya, K. Horiuchi, & K. Uchiyama (Eds.), *The Japanese economy: Social common capital and sustainable development*. Tokyo: University of Tokyo Press (in Japanese).

Kinzai Institute for Financial Affairs. (Ed.). (1959). *Growth potential of the Japanese economy: Shimomura theory and critique*. Tokyo: Financial Affairs (in Japanese).

Murakami, Y. (Ed.). (1971). *Economic growth: Readings, economic growth, No. 4*. Tokyo: Nihon Keizai Press (in Japanese).

Nakayama, I., & Economist. (Eds.). (1960). *Growth of the Japanese economy*. Tokyo: University of Tokyo Press (in Japanese).

Shimomura, O. (1951). Economic fluctuation and multiplier analysis. *Monthly Research Report, 40*(3), 61–89, *40*(5), 56–79, *40*(7), 1–86. Ministry of Finance (in Japanese).
Shimomura, O. (1955). A tight monetary policy: To understand it correctly. *Financial Affairs, 6*(1), 50–61 (in Japanese).
Shimomura, O. (1958). Realizing economic growth. In Kochikai. (Ed.). *Realizing economic growth.* Tokyo: Kochikai (in Japanese).
Shimomura, O. (1959a). The fundamentals of the Japanese economy and its growth potential: A critique of the excessive growth thesis and an examination of Japan's growth potential. *Financial Affairs, 10*(9), 19–25 (in Japanese).
Shimomura, O. (1959b). Growth theory and the growth potential of the Japanese economy. In Kinzai Institute for Financial Affairs. (Ed.), *The Growth potential of the Japanese economy.* Tokyo: Kinzai Institute for Financial Affairs (in Japanese).
Shimomura, O. (1961a). Basic issues on growth policy. *Quarterly Theoretical Economics, 11*(3–4), 1–15 (in Japanese).
Shimomura, O. (1961b). The current economic conditions and how to deal with them. *Financial Affairs, 12*(24), 18–28 (in Japanese).
Shimomura, O. (1962). *A theory of Japanese economic growth.* Tokyo: Kinzai Institute for Financial Affairs (in Japanese).
Shimomura, O. (1965). The advocates of stable growth defeated! *Business, Toyo Keizai Press, 9*(7), 8–27 (in Japanese).
Shimomura, O. (1971). *Options for Japan as economic giant: Collected papers*. Tokyo: Toyo Keizai Press (in Japanese).
Uzawa, H. (1991). In memory of Shimomura-san. In Compilation committee in honor of Dr. Shimomura (Eds.), *Osamu Shimonura* (in Japanese).

Chapter 4
Vision of Zero Growth and Performance After the Oil Crisis

Abstract We selected five papers by Dr. Shimomura and analyzed important issues such as his vision of zero-growth, policies to stabilize low-growth economy, discipline and equilibrium, Reaganomics, and bubble economy. When the oil crisis broke out in 1973, Dr. Shimomura suddenly changed his vision of high growth (10% a year) to zero-growth (1–2% a year). This change in forecast surprised the business community of Japan. Dr. Shimomura urged them to prepare for a zero growth. Dr. Shimomura warned that the fiscal and monetary policies cannot completely resolve the economic problems. He emphasized that consumers, labor unions, businesses, banks, and the government should exercise discipline to stabilize zero growth. In this case, discipline implies that stakeholders of an economy should take into consideration the whole scenario and exercise self-control. Dr. Shimomura emphasized maintaining a balanced budget. He criticized the US Reaganomics in the 1980s and Japan's bubble economy in the second half of 1980s. As the data analysis shows, the zero growth vision was right. If some special and unsustainable reasons are excluded, then it can be seen that Japan witnessed an annual growth rate of almost 1–2% for 40 years since the oil crisis. The keywords that Dr. Shimomura thought important in a zero growth economy are innovation, equilibrium, and discipline.

Keywords Zero-growth · Discipline · Equilibrium · National economy · Voluntary export restraints

4.1 Unrest in the World Economy

The advanced economies in the 1960s experienced a steady growth under the IMF–GATT system. This system worked well when the US economy was overwhelmingly strong and competitive. However, since the second half of the 1960s, economic power of the US began to decline relatively and it was difficult to maintain

K. Horiuchi and M. Otaki, *Dr. Osamu Shimomura's Legacy and the Postwar Japanese Economy*, Development Bank of Japan Research Series,
DOI 10.1007/978-981-10-5762-5_4

this system. In addition, economic growth of the advanced nations was causing new problems such as the exhaustion of oil resources and industrial pollution damage.

At the beginning of the 1970s, the world economy was shocked twice and became unstable.

In 1973, the fixed exchange rate system of IMF was abandoned and the flexible exchange rate system was introduced. Under the flexible exchange system, foreign exchange rates began to fluctuate drastically and sometimes led to a state of misalignment in which market rates deviated from the purchasing power parity. Moreover, with the liberalization of the international capital, the fiscal and monetary policies of a big nation like the US influenced the world economy through changes in interest rates and foreign exchange rates. This was the case of the Reaganomics in the 1980s.

The first oil crisis in October 1973 caused another economic setback. The world crude oil prices, which had been stable at $2 per barrel, suddenly quadrupled. The second oil crises that took place in 1979 had more than doubled the price of crude oil. This oil shock produced severe effects on world economy including Japan.

There were serious problems such as sluggish economic growth, cost-push inflation, unemployment, deficit of the government budget, and deterioration of the balance of payments.

The Japanese economy was influenced seriously by these two shocks. High growth period was over. The Japanese economy as well as other advanced economies entered the low growth period.

The Japanese economy plunged into a period of low growth from high growth in the 1970s. The annual rate of economic growth of Japan was approximately 4% from 1970 to 1980. During this period, lower economic growth was witnessed across the globe. However, if we assume that the Japanese economy must have been compatible with the stable world economies, then we will understand that the rate of growth of the Japanese economy should have been much lower than 4%. We will examine this point later. In the first half of the 1990s, economic recession was prolonged and the Japanese economy virtually recorded "zero growth."

In this context, in Chap. 4, we will choose five papers by Dr. Shimomura and explain why he changed his vision of the Japanese economy from high growth to "zero growth" in 1974. We will also analyze the factors essential for stabilizing "zero growth" as per Dr. Shimomura and summarize his five disciplines that should be observed by economic agents. This analysis will help us understand that his economic perspective is based on political economy, which aims at developing national economy.

The Japanese economy, since 1970, will be divided into four periods: the adjustment period after the oil shock in the 1970s, shock period due to Reaganomics in the first half of the 1980s, bubble economy period in the second half of the 1980s, and starting period of zero growth in the first half of the 1990s.

4.2 Vision of Zero Growth

Around 1970, the Japanese economy caught up with those of European countries, and economists indicated that the country might witness a possible deceleration in its high growth rate. The oil crisis broke out in 1973 and caused serious confusion in the world economy. Japan was compelled to adjust its economy to be able to respond to this serious shock. Dr. Shimomura expressed his new vision of "zero growth" in 1974.

The critical factor was the oil crisis in 1973. The oil crisis gave a serious setback to Japan because the country depended heavily on crude oil imports. Dr. Shimomura recognized that a limited oil supply would destroy one of the fundamental conditions for favorable global economic growth, and the Japanese economy would fail to maintain internal and external equilibrium conditions simultaneously. His growth theory consistently focused on equilibrium conditions.

It was only after a few months of the outbreak of the oil crisis that Dr. Shimomura announced zero growth. He considered oil a critically important factor of production. Economists and businesspersons were interested in the growth rate figures, and their arguments on the subject led them to speculate whether the growth rate would be 4, 5, or 6%. However, Dr. Shimomura was not interested in these figures and asserted that the growth rate would be "zero." His concern was not a growth rate but a new vision after the oil crisis.

(*Paper 1*)

Soon after the oil crisis, in January 1974, Dr. Shimomura published a paper titled "*Japanese economy is on a zero-growth track*," in which he clearly expressed his vision of zero growth for the Japanese economy.

The vision of zero growth implied a sudden and discontinuous change in the growth path from 10 to 1–2% per annum at the most. He regarded 1–2% growth as "zero." The assertions in this paper shocked the business community in particular. He (1974) wrote as follows.

> The oil crisis seems to have definitively derailed the growth trajectory of the Japanese economy. Japan is no longer on the high growth track it was on in the past; it is not even on a stable growth trajectory, let alone a high growth one. It now appears that the Japanese economy has been pushed off a growth trajectory and onto a zero-growth one. ... This means that we need to be prepared to enter an era of long-term zero growth. Of course, Japan may not literally see zero growth, as energy-saving innovations will surely produce some growth. There could be developments in alternative energy as well. Also, the development of oil resources worldwide will probably continue to go ahead, and it is unlikely that oil supplies from producer countries will reach their absolute limit. Nevertheless, the Japanese economy will certainly need to survive under conditions where the oil supply is extremely tight. In broad terms, this will not allow even a stable growth, let alone high growth. Only minimal growth will be possible. This prospect is certain. We have no other choice but to prepare for it.
>
> [Shimomura (1974), "Japanese economy is on a zero-growth track"]

Dr. Shimomura urged business community to prepare for zero growth and used the word "prepare" two times in a short paragraph.

Japanese people were surprised by his zero-growth vision and discussed his changes in logic. However, Dr. Shimomura had not changed his basic logic. There was a change in the condition that had been the basis for global economic growth of the world—cheap and abundant supply of oil. However, the fact that he suddenly changed his vision from high growth to "zero growth" greatly surprised the stakeholders of the Japanese economy.

There were several reasons why people did not agree with Dr. Shimomura. They considered zero growth gloomy—it implied zero corporate growth and zero increase in income. It was difficult for people who were used to high growth to accept this new vision. A zero growth economy is a slow-paced economy. Dr. Shimomura emphasized, "If we change thinking and adjust our life, zero growth won't be gloomy. The Japanese economy will be like European economy."

In addition to these general feelings, people thought that there are always pessimists and optimists in the world, and that Dr. Shimomura simply shifted from an optimistic view to a pessimistic view. However, people did not realize that Dr. Shimomura did not change his logic.

Generally, most economists were not so serious. There were several reasons. They pointed out that the ratio of oil consumption to GDP was low, and this ratio would protect the Japanese economy from serious damage from the oil shock. However, oil is a basic material that is used directly and indirectly for the production of goods and services. The above argument overlooked this important point. Dr. Shimomura often said, "We can't grow rice without oil."

Another argument was that although the oil crisis posed a major problem, it would have a temporary effect on the economy. Thus, Japan would recover from the shock and the economy would resume its growth path after a few years. The growth rate might be less than 10%, but it would be higher than that of Europe and the US. Most economists and political leaders supported this view. They indicated that the Japanese economy has an excellent ability to change. Therefore, economic growth would not slow down drastically.

Contrarily, Dr. Shimomura warned that high capacity would not bring about domestic demand-led growth, as in the 1960s. He believed that although Japanese firms increase their productivity, this would not lead to an increase in domestic demand, because it was restricted by the constrained oil supply. In addition, he believed that labor-saving innovations would have a destabilizing effect on adjustment process. He was also concerned with the unemployment problem.

Instead of labor-saving innovations, Dr. Shimomura emphasized the promotion of innovation for the development of new products, new sources of energy, pollution prevention, environmental conservation, and human health. Additionally, innovations for saving oil consumption will contribute toward easing the oil supply constraints. Dr. Shimomura believed that investments of firms should be directed to develop innovations that can facilitate the establishment of a sustainable society.

The government expressed an optimistic view. According to the mid-term economic outlook of the government, the rate of economic growth was expected to be 6% per annum in the Economic Plan of 1976–1980 and 5.7% per annum in the Economic Plan of 1979–1985. In 1978, Dr. Shimomura expressed his opinion on government's plans; he pointed out that the annual growth rate projection of 6% was far from reality and that growth rate cannot exceed 2–3%. The government continued to increase public expenditure to increase the growth rate, which deteriorated the fiscal balance. A surge in public investments disrupted the natural environment. The maintenance of a balanced government budget was one of the disciplines emphasized by Dr. Shimomura.

4.3 Discipline

In the 1960s, Shimomura supported the principle of free and unrestricted activities of the entrepreneur. This principle promoted rapid changes and improvements in the standard of living of the Japanese people. However, after the oil crisis the Japanese economy was restricted by limited oil supplies. It was difficult to adapt to the oil crisis and adjust to a zero-growth economy. The principles that were effective during the high-growth period were no longer useful in a slow-paced economy and were expected to disrupt the adjustment process.[1]

(*Paper 2*)

In 1976, Dr. Shimomura delivered a lecture in commemoration of the 25th anniversary of the Japan Development Bank. The title of the lecture was "*Japanese Economy: Challenges and Future Choices.*" In this lecture, he expressed his view that fiscal and monetary policies cannot resolve all the economic problems that might emerge during Japan's transition from a high growth to zero growth economy. His lecture (1976) is as follows.

> The first challenge we are facing today is how to overcome the adjustment problems caused by the transition from high to low growth. These problems are unavoidable and will be accompanied by tremendous pain, but we have no choice but to endure that pain and overcome it.
>
> The second challenge is to free ourselves as soon as possible from the patterns of behavior and the ways of thinking of the high-growth period. We need to make efforts to get used to, and adapt to, low growth.
>
> It is widely believed that the reason the current recession has persisted for two years, and still has not been overcome, is due to the government's poor policies. Many believe that the

[1]Dr. Shimomura (1978) states, "After the oil crisis, we have to adapt ourselves to the economic problems at a slow tempo. Fortunate or not, this change occurred as a historical condition. We have no other choice but to adapt ourselves to this new condition and to find clever ways to fulfill our life privately and socially to the maximum extent.".

economy will recover if the government skillfully manages fiscal and monetary policy. … I believe, however, that this is a huge mistake.

… If high growth were to continue, fiscal and monetary policies, although not all-powerful, would certainly be effective in solving most, if not all, the problems we face. However, the hard fact is that such policies are virtually powerless against the problems that emerge during the transition from high to low growth.

… Some say that because low economic growth will make it difficult to mitigate unemployment, improve social welfare and maintain our living conditions, Japan needs a higher growth rate. This is similar to the idea of a "necessary growth rate". The idea of a "necessary growth rate" is based on an assumption that the economic growth rate can be determined by freely choosing whatever rate we like. This belief that even the growth rate can be freely selected as long as fiscal and monetary policies are managed skillfully is essentially the idea that fiscal and monetary policy is a cure-all.

… We have to make the transition from high to low growth. We have no other choice but to do our very best within the limitations of our situation. No matter how painful, we must endure. …

… Once we overcome all these impediments, while Japan will have a low growth rate, it will be in a stable and steady economic state—and will be more affluent than ever before in its history.

[Shimomura (1976), "Japanese Economy: Challenges and Future Choices"]

In this lecture, he mentioned that we should change the behavioral pattern and the way of thinking that emerged during the high growth period.

The Japanese economy had to make a sudden transition from rapid growth to zero growth state. The economy was undergoing a severe adjustment process, and it had to be realized with minimal disturbance. The people of Japan had to change their mindset and behavior. The moral obligation that Dr. Shimomura referred to as "discipline" was essential for stabilizing a zero growth economy.

Discipline is a kind of code of conduct. According to Dr. Shimomura (1987b), economic agents should exercise discipline by considering the effect of their behavior on the economy as a whole and employing self-control when deciding on economic actions. In this sense, it seems that Dr. Shimomura's "discipline" corresponds to A. Smith's "sympathy" in *the Theory of Moral Sentiment*.

It should be noted that the keywords of Dr. Shimomura's vision underwent a change. The keywords that expressed a high-growth period were innovation, equilibrium, and freedom with self-responsibility. However, the keywords for a zero-growth period comprised innovation, equilibrium, and discipline. Freedom with self-responsibility was replaced by discipline. According to Dr. Shimomura, the era of *laissez faire* was over. Economic agents were expected to act according to discipline. For more details, please see Horiuchi (2007, 2014).

Dr. Shimomura emphasized that consumers, labor unions, businesses, banks, and the government must exercise discipline to stabilize zero growth. He was of the opinion that implementation of moral principle, as expressed below, was important for achieving long-term equilibrium. In this sense, it was essential for economic agents to undertake prudent activities. In summary, Dr. Shimomura wrote the following about discipline since 1974 (See Shimomura and Suzuki (1978)):

<Discipline by Shimomura>

(a) Consumers should appreciate the fact that they are leading more affluent lifestyles than ever, and hence should refrain from trying to get more. They should not overemphasize on procuring material possesions.
(b) Labor unions should exercise self-control and should not demand wage increases.
(c) Businesses should exercise self-control by not investing in labor-saving innovations and capacity-expansion projects. However, investments to save energy should be encouraged.
(d) Banks should observe monetary discipline and exercise self-control regarding while undertaking speculative activities.
(e) The Government should maintain fiscal discipline or a balanced budget.

The need for exercising discipline was important at that time, especially in the aftermath of oil crisis. However, discipline is still important in a zero growth economy. What happened after the oil crisis in the context of discipline? We will briefly examine the economic performance from 1970 to 1980.

Concerning the consumers, Dr. Shimomura believed that they should be satisfied with their material life and should look inward to achieve inner enhancement. In a zero growth economy, he expected that people would try to attain a more sophisticated lifestyle, which reminds us of what J. S. Mill described about lifestyle of people in a stationary state. However, it seems that value change of consumers from high growth to zero growth did not occur. In addition, we experienced the bubble economy in the second half of the 1980s.

Concerning the labor unions, Dr. Shimomura believed that in a zero growth economy, wage increase would cause cost-push inflation and consequently lead to stagnant economies. Labor unions demanded higher wages and wages jumped up in 1974. An increase in wages and a hike in the oil prices pushed up production costs and firms began to invest in labor-saving technologies.[2] However, labor unions refrained from demanding higher wages to protect employment during the second oil crisis in 1980. Therefore, except for the unusual case in 1974, the wage increase did not cause cost-push inflation in Japan.

Concerning the businesses, a firm can become more competitive if it succeeds in increasing labor productivity. However, increasing labor productivity in a zero-growth economy will tend to increase unemployment. Therefore, working hours should be reduced to avoid unemployment. In fact, a hike in oil prices stimulates a firm to invest for increasing labor productivity. Cut-throat competition among firms took roots during the high growth period, and the domestic market remained very competitive after the oil crisis. However, the domestic market was kept in a state of "zero growth." Firms tried to increase labor productivity to reduce costs, looked for new markets in Europe and the US, and increased exports rapidly.

---

[2]If there had not been large hikes in wages in 1974, then an increase in labor productivity might have led to a reduction of working hours.

Export-oriented growth became a political issue with other countries. The external balance of Japan showed a large trade surplus. The appreciation of yen in the second half of the 1980s and 1990s compelled firms to increase labor productivity and led companies to move their production plants to foreign countries through foreign direct investment (FDI).

Dr. Shimomura expected Japanese firms to refrain from engaging in cut-throat competition and increasing labor productivity in a zero growth economy. However, his expectation was not realized.

An innovation should make a meaningful contribution to a firm and a society. Dr. Shimomura insisted that energy saving and alternative energy projects would be meaningful investments. Discipline in business requires a firm not to engage in cut-throat competition, but to emphasize corporate social responsibility (CSR).

Concerning banks, in the second half of 1980s, financial institutions lost monetary discipline, which caused excess liquidity and resulted in bubble economy. We will examine bubble economy later. Financial institutions should recognize the essence of the present monetary system. Unlike gold standard, in the present-day currency system, money supply depends on human judgment.[3]

Of the four disciplines, Shimomura emphasized most on fiscal discipline. However, the government's expansionary policy resulted in massive accumulation of national bonds. The government pursued domestic demand growth policies to maintain employment levels and reduce the trade surplus. The government used expansionary policy that led to massive issues of national bonds. The long-term equilibrium conditions were not met. The principle of a balanced budget was abandoned in 1975 and the fiscal balance fell into deficit.

1. Discipline and equilibrium

Dr. Shimomura emphasized macroeconomic equilibrium. However, after the oil crisis, the internal balance (deficit of fiscal balance) and external balance (surplus of current balance) were in a state of disequilibrium.

In a zero-growth economy, if a firm introduces innovation to increase labor productivity, keeping the nominal wages constant, then there would be a decline in prices and deflationary pressure might prevail in the domestic market. This will cause an increase in exports and result in the appreciation of the yen rate in the long-run. Under these circumstances, the government's policy to deregulate labor market with an aim of increasing non-regular workers will strengthen the aforementioned problem of deflationary pressure.[4] We will discuss the problems of labor market deregulation in Chap. 5.

[3]Dr. Shimomura told in his private study circle that, in a zero-growth economy, short-term interest would be zero and long-term interest would be 1–2% at the most.

[4]If misalignment of exchange rate occurs in the international financial market and the yen rate appreciates for some time, then a firm will try to increase labor productivity. However, the firms will not agree to increase the wages. Misalignment of exchange rate will disturb equilibrium relationship between price, wage, and productivity.

In this sense, there will be a possibility that internal equilibrium (stable prices) and external equilibrium (balanced current account) are not sustained in macro economy. The disciplines of Dr. Shimomura are the basis of and firmly connected to macroeconomic equilibrium in a "zero growth" era. "To think of the whole and control the self" is a rational code of conduct of each economic agent.[5]

2. Exhaustible resources

Pertaining to the oil crisis, other issues emerged during the period. It is true that the adaptive capacity of Japanese firms to the oil crisis was considerably high, but this did not increase the domestic demand by the private sector. The government kept stimulating domestic demand, and the economy followed a different path that was above the trajectory of "zero growth." This was one of the reasons why the zero growth vision was not accepted by economists, businesspersons, and political leaders.

Additionally, the people in Japan were under the impression that the oil crisis was over. The oil price fell considerably in the first half of 1980s. Subsequently, there was a gradual rise in the oil prices; however, yen appreciated in the latter half of the 1980s. Thus, the price of imported oil in terms of yen did not rise from the mid-1980s to the mid 1990s.

Contrarily, the world oil price in terms of the US dollars tended to rise in the long-term. The rate of increase over the period 1970–1996 was 9.7% per annum, which was almost equal to the average yield of the triple A-rated bonds of the US companies (see Fig. 4.1). The market indicated the exhaustibility of oil resources. However, the scenario might have indicated the end of the oil crisis period because sometimes supply exceeds demand in the world oil market. This is because the Japanese economy made utmost efforts to save energy and adjust to the oil supply constraints. Dr. Shimomura expected that the demand for oil in the developing countries, such as China and India, would increase and resultant constraints of oil supply would influence the world economy.

At present, there is an argument that oil, liquefied natural gas (LNG), shale oil, and other fossil energy are abundant. However, we should take into consideration the worsening global environmental issues and be careful with how much we can utilize fossil energy. We will need to regulate fossil fuel consumption by means of tax system and direct control for the public benefit. Energy saving activities must be enforced and accelerated more than ever. In order to restrict our economic activities within natural material cycle, our economy will have to be controlled within the upper limit of usable oil and fossil energy.

---

[5]A common approach to cope with global environmental issues is usually to "think globally and act locally.".

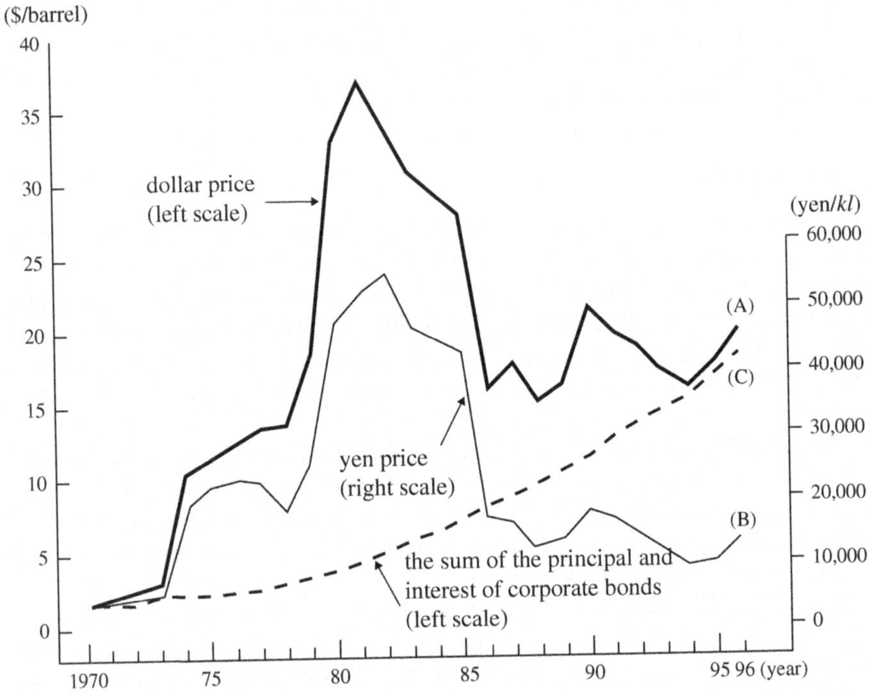

Fig. 4.1 Average price of imported crude oil. *Note* (1) Base year is 1970 when average price of imported crude oil was $1.81/barrel. (2) Yields on corporate bonds were those of AAA of Moody's. *Source* Ministry of Finance "Customs statistics", FRB "Federal Reserve Bulletin" Horiuchi (1998)

4.4 Performance After the Oil Crisis: 1971–1982

After the oil crisis, the Japanese economy experienced stagflation. People were very concerned about the future of the economy. There was a surge in prices and speculative movements occurred among consumers and business community. The Japanese firms began to increase exports, and the economy began to recover, expanding by around 3–5% annually. However, this growth pattern was different from what was experienced in the 1960s.

Growth rate declined considerably after the first oil crisis in 1973. Immediately after the crisis, the import value recorded a significant increase, and the current account fell into large deficit. Additionally, inflation posed a problem, and it was very difficult to maintain the internal and external equilibrium.

From 1971 to 1982, economic growth rate decreased to 4.2% per annum and exports increased to 8.9% per annum, which was twice the economic growth rate. An increase in exports played a critical role in boosting the Japanese economy. The

Table 4.1 Summary of the Japanese economy after the oil crisis

Annual rate of growth (%)	(1971–1982)	(1983–1985)	(1986–1990)	(1991–1996)
GDP (in real term)	4.2	3.5	4.6	1.4
Investment (in real terms)	2.6	8.4	10	−2.4
Export (in real term)	8.9	8.2	3	4.3
Current balance/GDP (%)	0.6	2.7	2.8	2.6

Source Table 3.2

average ratio of current account balance to nominal GDP was 0.6% and the Japanese economy attained external equilibrium (see Table 4.1).

In the high growth period, an increase in domestic demand facilitated the realization of economic growth. After the oil crisis, an increase in exports was responsible for pushing up the Japanese economy. Exports to the US and Europe showed a rapid increase, which was criticized as "intense deluge" of Japanese exports. The world economy was stagnant after the oil crisis and a rapid increase in Japanese exports caused political problems abroad.

Manufacturing industries, such as iron and steel, color television, and passenger cars, restricted their exports to the US and Europe to mitigate trade friction. This is called as voluntary export restrictions (VERs). VERs are trade agreements and a kind of controlled trade. VERs began to induce Japanese firms to increase foreign direct investment (FDI).

The rate of increase of private investment decreased to 2.6% annum from 18.4% per annum during the high growth period. Without an aggressive increase in exports, an increase in private investment would have been much smaller. Therefore, the entrepreneurs lost confidence and changed their investment motives; they shifted their focus from increasing capacity to increasing energy savings, rationalization, and labor savings.

Concerning the internal equilibrium, the Japanese economy had two problems. The first problem was posed by inflation. From 1973 to 1975, cost-push inflation occurred. This was attributed to an increase in wages after the first oil crisis. During the second oil crisis in 1979, the labor unions refrained from demanding a wage increase. They exercised self-restraint by not demanding compensation for oil price increase.

From 1971 to 1982, the oil prices went up and the wholesale prices (prices of industrial goods) increased to 6.5% per annum, while they were stable during the high growth period. During this period, the increase in labor productivity and nominal wages were 5.8% per annum and 11.6%, respectively. The unit labor costs (wage in terms of efficiency unit) also witnessed a surge during this period.

The second problem was attributed to the deterioration of fiscal balance. Since the second half of the 1970s, positive fiscal and monetary policies were implemented to help economy recover from recession and to achieve a moderate growth. Public investment for social infrastructure increased considerably. In fact, the government's economic plan aimed at 6% growth. As a result, the government started to issue deficit-covering bonds in 1975. Dr. Shimomura warned that it would be difficult to attain even a moderate growth; he also pointed out that the fiscal and monetary policies would not serve as solutions to all the economic problems.

The two oil crises put severe restrictions on the Japanese economy. External equilibrium was achieved during the 10-year period, but the increase in exports caused trade conflicts with the US and Europe. Internal equilibrium was not attained and fiscal deficit was financed through a large-scale issue of government bonds.

4.5 Reaganomics: 1983–1985

During a span of 10 years, starting in 1980, the Japanese economy was drawn into the vortex of Reaganomics. In the first half of the 1980s, Japanese export to the US increased very rapidly due to expansionary policy of the US government, which boosted the Japanese economy. After the Plaza Accord signed by the G-5 nations in 1985, the dollar rate declined and the yen rate registered a sharp increase in value. In order to cope with a higher yen, the Japanese government resorted to an easy money policy that triggered an asset bubble, consequently increasing the stock and land prices and expanding the Japanese economy further.

As discussed below, in the 1980s, Dr. Shimomura sharply criticized Reaganomics and Japanese policy. He also warned about the outbreak of the bubble economy. Dr. Shimomura's economic theory was based on the belief that each country should maintain disciplinary policy for establishing a stable and sustainable national economy.

From the 1950s through the first half of the 1960s, the US economy experienced a stable growth rate of 4% per annum (see Table 4.2). The prices were stable and interest rates were low. The current account was in surplus, and the budget of federal government was almost balanced. The economy had attained an internal and external equilibrium. However, in the second half of the 1960s, the US economy witnessed instability. The hollowing out of the manufacturing industries in the US began to attract attention. The industries in the US began to lose international competitiveness, and the Johnson administration implemented the "great society" policy to increase expenditure on "butter (welfare) and guns (Vietnam War)."

In the 1970s, the problem of imbalance became clearer. The most important event was the collapse of the Bretton Woods system. The US dollar was no longer a key currency, but was used as the most important international currency. The US government changed its traditional stance and chose to keep economic disciplines. The deficit in the government budget increased, economic growth rate registered a decline, and the wage-price spiral worsened further.

Imbalance in the US macro economy was apparent in the 1980s. This imbalance was primarily attributed to the practice of the "supply-side economics" by the Reagan administration. Reagan's policy was characterized by large-scale tax cuts, increased defense spending, cuts in other expenditures, and deregulation. The goal of Reaganomics was to have a small government and stimulate private sector-led

Table 4.2 Long-term trend of the US economy and consequences of Reaganomics (Annual average, %)

	1950–1959	1960–1969	1970–1979	1980–1988	1980–1983	1984–1985	1986–1988
Growth rate of real GDP	3.9	4.1	2.8	2.5	0.7	5.1	3.4
Increase rate of wholesale price	2.4	1.1	8.4	3.8	7.5	1.3	0.8
Increase rate of consumer price	2.1	2.3	7.1	5.6	8.2	3.9	3.2
Operating rate (manufacturing)	83.7	84.9	80.9	78.5	75.4	80.3	81.4
Personal saving rate	6.8	6.7	8.0	5.5	6.7	5.4	3.9
Unemployment rate	4.4	4.7	6.1	7.4	8.4	7.3	6.1
Yield of 10-year gov. bond	3.2	4.7	7.5	10.8	12.4	11.5	8.3
Ratio of trade balance to nominal GNP	0.7	0.7	−0.5	−2.3	−1.2	−3.0	−3.2
Ratio of current balance to nominal GNP	0.1	0.5	0.0	−1.8	−0.4	−2.9	−3.2
Ratio of federal gov. deficit to nominal GNP	−0.4	−0.8	−2.2	−4.2	−4.0	−5.2	−4.0

Source US Government, *Economic Report of the President*
Office of Management and Budget (OMB), *Historical Tables*
Horiuchi (1998)

economic growth. Reagan's initial plan focused on balancing the government budget, as economic growth was expected to realize an increase in tax revenue.

Reaganomics was started in 1981. The US government implemented a bold and expansionary fiscal policy, while the Federal Reserve Board (FRB) implemented a stringent monetary policy to control persistent inflation. This extreme policy mix had a serious impact on the macroeconomic equilibrium. Internal disequilibrium (government budget deficit) markedly expanded, which enlarged external disequilibrium (current account deficit), and the resulting twin deficits posed a serious problem.

Reaganomics had a serious impact on the world economy. In international trade, countries across the globe, including Japan, increased exports to the US. In international finance, the high interest rate of the US spread to other countries. The real interest rate of major countries remained very high. In the first half of the 1980s, the dollar appreciated and remained in a state of serious misalignment.

In the 1980s, the Japanese government was trying to decrease its fiscal deficits to balance its budget, while the Japanese economy was affected by an abrupt economic tsunami created by the US economy.

From 1983 to 1985, the US dollar appreciated to other currencies. A dollar was 227, 249, and 239 yen in 1980, 1982, and 1985, respectively. The dollar was kept overvalued. The effect of Reaganomics was clearly seen in Japanese exports to the US. In 1982, the current account surplus was 0.7% of nominal GDP. However, in 1985 it increased sharply to 3.6%. An increase in exports to the US reached 79% of the total increase in the Japanese exports.

From 1983 to 1985, the exports increased to 8.2% per annum (see Table 4.1). An increase in exports induced private investment, which increased to 8.4% per annum. Firms competed to invest in plant and equipment, which was referred to as high tech investment, to produce microelectronics products. High tech investment had an economy of scale or increasing returns of scale. A learning effect realized by an increased export of high tech products increased labor productivity and led to trade conflicts between Japan and the US. Therefore, VERs were introduced to resolve the trade conflicts.

In Japan, the government started to restore fiscal balance in 1980. The expenditures were curtailed and public investment decreased 4.1% per annum from 1983 to 1985 (see Table 3.2) to achieve a balanced budget. Public sector balance was 2.4% in deficit in 1982. Due to export-led economic growth, tax revenues increased and public sector balance improved to 0.2% in surplus in 1985, which was an improvement of 2.6 points (see Table 4.3).

Exports to the US increased, which stimulated investment-led growth. As a result, savings increased in the private and public sectors. There was a causal relationship from investment increase to savings increase and not the other way around. The Japanese economy was set to restore fiscal balance. There was no change in the economic policy of Japan and there was a sudden increase in exports to the US. The Japanese economy simply responded to changes in the economic policy of the US.

Table 4.3 Balance of investment and savings in Japan (%)

Calendar year	1982	1985	1990	1995
Private sector balance	3.0	3.4	-2.6	4.5
Savings	27.1	26.8	24.7	26.7
Investment	24.1	23.4	27.3	22.1
Household balance	8.1	8.1	4.7	7.1
Savings	16.5	15.3	12.4	13.9
Investment	8.4	7.2	7.8	6.7
Corporate balance	−5.1	−4.7	−7.3	−2.6
Savings	10.6	11.6	12.3	12.8
Investment	15.7	16.3	19.5	15.4
Public sector balance	−2.4	0.2	3.9	−2.3
Savings	3.4	4.9	8.9	4.1
Investment	5.8	4.7	5.0	6.4
Foreign sector balance	0.7	3.6	1.3	2.2
Export	16.5	16.3	15.0	13.4
Import	15.8	12.7	13.7	11.2
Nominal GDP	100.0	100.0	100.0	100.0

Source Economic Planning Agency "Annual Statistics on National Economy"

The above is a summary of Dr. Shimomura's analysis of Reaganomics and its effect on the Japanese economy. In short, Japan was not responsible for the sudden increase in exports to the US. However, many Japanese and American economists insisted that as Japan's savings exceeded its investment, it should formulate a policy to increase domestic demand for increasing imports and decreasing the trade surplus. In 1980s, the US government often demanded Japan to increase domestic demand.

Dr. Shimomura objected to such policy as it would have required the Japanese government to increase public investment, which would deteriorate fiscal balance in a zero-growth economy.

(*Paper 3*)

Dr. Shimomura criticized the large tax cuts by the Reagan administration. According to supply-side economics of Reaganomics, a tax cut will increase savings, which will increase investment and productivity and finally facilitate the realization of economic growth. This would lead to an increase in tax revenues and restoration of the fiscal balance. In response to this argument, Dr. Shimomura pointed out that a tax-cut would not induce economic growth that would be large enough to attain a balanced budget. He also insisted that an increase in savings would decrease effective demand and lower economic growth.

In Reaganomics, the supply-side economics would resolve all the economic problems, and thereby enable the fiscal policy to determine the rate of economic growth. Shimomura (1981) published a book ("*Discipline and the Japanese Economy*") and criticized the supply-side economics in the following words.

> The reason why American economic thought has totally lost its influence today, is that American economists have focused only on managing demand, believing that everything else would work out from there. … Supply-side economics is now beginning to be actively discussed. This way of thinking is based on the idea that when considering real economic conditions, it is not enough to only manage demand. One should also consider what would create the conditions for an increase in supply. Judging from the economic policies that have surfaced under President Reagan, however, it seems that even those American economists that are considering supply-side economics do not yet grasp the essence of economic growth. … For these economists 'supply' is just a word. They claim that supply increases are essentially a matter of increasing innovation or improving productivity, through tax reductions. But increasing productivity is not that simple. They fail to recognize the importance of the entire nation's attitude towards work and their desire to improve productivity – in other words, they do not recognize that productivity has a human dimension.
>
> This point becomes clear if we consider the case of Japan during its high growth era. During its high economic growth period, Japan increased government revenue through tax reductions. However, to be precise, government revenue increased despite tax reductions. … It so happened that the Japanese economy at the time already had the necessary conditions for high growth. In this environment, the government was able to reduce taxes because of growth. Tax reductions were merely a means of maintaining a fiscal position adequate to facilitate high growth. It certainly is not the case that high growth came as a result of the tax reduction.
>
> [Shimomura (1981), "Discipline and the Japanese Economy"]

Dr. Shimomura firmly believed that economic growth cannot be attained simply through tax cuts. Economic growth reflects the willingness and energy of a nation.

Dr. Shimomura criticized Reaganomics and blamed it for destroying the stability of the US economy, and the internal and external equilibrium. In addition, Reaganomics was primarily responsible for instability in the world economy—high interest rates and misalignment of exchange rates.

The large Japanese trade surplus with the US triggered a macroeconomic debate and trade conflicts. The US economic policy toward Japan had two objectives. First, Japan should realize domestic demand-led economic growth. Second, Japan should promote economic restructuring to increase access of the US firms and investors to the Japanese market.

The Maekawa Report was published in 1986. This report was written by Prime Minister Nakasone's private committee to suggest the Japanese government to promote policies such as the promotion of domestic demand, increasing access to Japanese market, and deregulation of banking and securities sectors. In short, this report was in consonance with the US intention. Many economists and policy makers in Japan repeatedly emphasized domestic demand-led economic growth and international coordination of macroeconomic policies. Dr. Shimomura rejected this view because a large surplus of trade balance of Japan with the US was a result of Reaganomics and not vice versa. In addition, according to his zero-growth vision, it was impossible to realize a domestic demand-led growth policy. This policy would deteriorate fiscal balance.

The structural impediments initiative (SII) was started in 1989 between Japan and the US. The US requested Japan to increase domestic demand by increasing public investment and to increase import by opening the Japanese semiconductors and car parts markets.

A policy to increase imports was referred to as the "voluntary import expansions (VIEs)." Dr. Shimomura was in favor of "VERs" as he regarded VERs as one of the disciplines of international trade under a zero growth world economy. VERs between Japan and the US would set a limit on Japanese exports, thereby ensuring that the employment stability of the import country (the US) is not disrupted. Japan and the US could keep GDP and employment at a constant and stable level. Dr. Shimomura opposed VIEs because they would increase employment of the export country (the US) at the cost of the import country (Japan). This policy would be similar to a "beggar-my-neighbor" policy in a zero-growth economy.

(*Paper 4*)

The global economic growth had slackened after the oil crisis. Considering these circumstances, VERs would have been preferable to VIEs for maintaining international trade stability. This was one of Dr. Shimomura's disciplines. His main emphasis was on the stability of the national economy during a zero-growth period. In this sense, he did not agree with free trade policy without reservations. He also insisted that the international coordination of macroeconomic policy must be based on the principle that each country should make efforts to prioritize sustaining disciplined domestic policies.

Commenting on the international coordination of macroeconomic policy, Dr. Shimomura used to say, "Japan is not to blame, but the US is to blame." Shimomura (1987b) published one of the best selling books ("*Japan is not to blame*") and criticized Reaganomics in the following words.

> What is the national economy? For Japan it is the question of how the 120 million people living in the archipelago eat and stay alive. These people cannot escape from the fate of living on the Japanese archipelago. This is the foundation of their existence. Those who escape overseas are exceptions. All of them are destined to live out their lives on our four main islands.
>
> How should 120 million people secure their employment, raise their income level and enjoy a stable life? That's the core of the national economy. Of course, Japan continues to strive to address these questions, as do all other nations around the world. It is only natural that various frictions will arise in the course of these efforts. And it is the international economy that should manage these frictions.
>
> For this reason, we pursue free trade in the hope that it will be mutually beneficial. … Every country has its minimum requirements that must be maintained to survive. A view of free trade that ignores this reality will only cause harm. … A critical error in the principle of free trade is that it lacks a perspective on the national economy.
>
> … It is therefore fundamentally important that each country takes responsibility for curing its own ills. In accordance with the principle of self-responsibility, each country must take responsibility for stabilizing its economy. … The United States is no exception. It is crucial

that it solves its own problems, rather than shifts the responsibility onto other countries. This is the only solution; there is no other way.

[Shimomura (1987b), "Japan is not to blame"]

In the 1960s, promoted by free trade, the world economy met the conditions for high growth. However, the world economy remained sluggish after the oil crisis. The use of VERs was the effective medium to facilitate industrial adjustment. VERs imposes trade restrictions and contributes to stabilizing and keeping economic order during industrial adjustment process. For example, VER on Japanese automobiles to the US would stabilize the foreign exchange rate. In general, stable exchange rates are very important for corporate planning. It is also very important for carrying out smooth changes in industrial structure and for stable employment of both export and import countries.

Shimomura did not support the idea of free trade and supported VERs to stabilize a zero-growth economy. Contrarily, VIEs, which the US government required Japan to implement, were like foreign policy that aimed at opening the Japanese market. This policy would decrease Japanese employment and increase the employment levels of the US, and hence must be a protective trade policy.

Dr. Shimomura emphasized that trade system should be judged from a point of view of national economy and realistic policies should be formulated, considering the zero-growth economy.

4.6 Bubble Economy: 1986–1990

From 1984 to 1985, the US economy expanded. Due to the twin deficits and low savings rate, the real interest rate remained high and appreciation of the dollar continued. After Plaza Accord was signed in 1985, a policy to correct dollar appreciation was initiated. The Japanese yen to a dollar started to appreciate immediately. It was 239, 169, 145, and 128 yen in 1985, 1986, 1987, and 1988, respectively.

The market rate approached purchasing power parity (PPP) of the machinery industry was most competitive in Japan (see Fig. 4.2). The sudden appreciation of the yen forced the Japanese firms to cut production costs. From 1985 to 1988, the labor productivity increased 17.5%, but the nominal wages increased only 7.8% in manufacturing industry. Those who worked hard to improve productivity were not rewarded properly.

Japan was set to reduce fiscal deficit. The government did not change fiscal policy and formulated a large-scale easy money policy to cope with the appreciation of the yen. The official discount rate of yen was 5% in 1986, which reduced successively to 2.5% in 1989. The easy money policy lowered interest rate in the market and led to an excessive supply of money. Banks lost monetary discipline, and speculation on stock and real estate was rampant. Consequently, the asset prices of stock and land increased, which triggered the bubble economy.

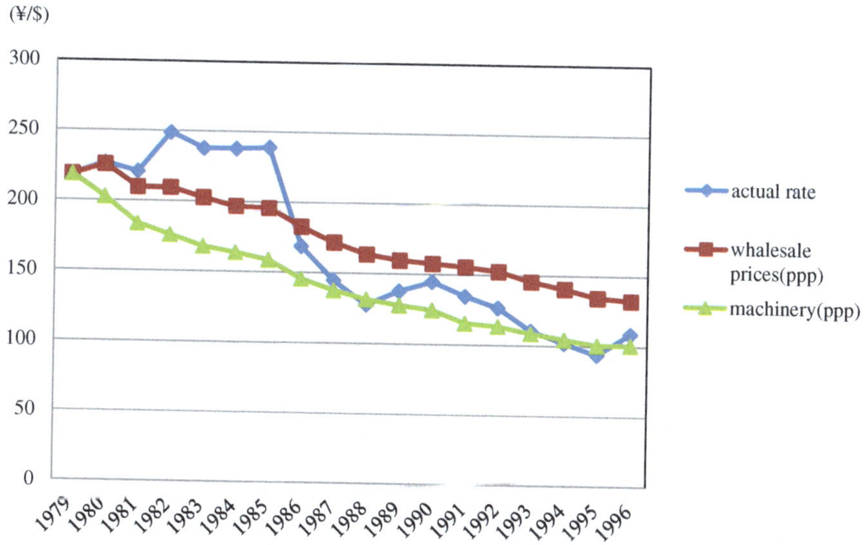

Fig. 4.2 Exchange rate (V$)—Actual rate and PPP. *Note* The base year of PPP is 1979 ($1 = ¥219). *Source* US Department of Labor "Bureau of Labor Statistics", Bank of Japan "Annual Report on Economic Statistics"

Owing to capital gains, people increased expenditure on expensive household appliances, such as large refrigerator and high-grade cars. A lower interest rate stimulated housing investment. An increase in consumption and housing investment stimulated corporate investment, which realized domestic demand-led growth. From 1986 to 1990, the annual rate of growth was 10.0% in corporate investment, 9.3% in housing investment, and 4.6% in GDP (see Table 3.2). The deficit financing government bonds, which had been issued from 1975, stopped in 1990. Both internal and external disequilibrium seemed corrected.

However, growth was realized under the influence of the bubble. Therefore, "expansion," instead of "growth," seemed to fit well during the period. The bubble-led economic expansion was not stable and the bubble collapsed in 1990.

(*Paper 5*)

From the beginning, Shimomura (1987a) was very critical of the bubble economy and published a paper ("*Zaitech will destroy enterprise*") as follows.

> The boom of zaitech and 'money games' seems to have led people to think that making money by managing money is good, while hard work is a fool's game. This is very troubling. It seems to me that the media is either trying to destroy the people's idea of the economy or is doing its best to erode Japan's economic stability. …
>
> It is inherently impossible to make money from money. While it may look as if money is making money, this is in fact an illusion. The origin of such an illusion is the financial system. The system of increasing money through credit creation can make it appear as though money is producing more money. …

> … If everybody became enthusiastic about money games and devoted themselves to them, the world would simply collapse. … Some compare this serious situation to the Great Depression of 1929. Certainly, at that time the US economy was inflated, just like a money game. Unlike today, however, there was still an effective brake on this inflation, as the economy was tied to the gold standard. … A bubble has to burst sometime. … In this sense, the situation today is far more serious than it was in 1929.
>
> [Shimomura (1987a), "Zaitech will destroy enterprise"]

1. "Zero-growth"

In summing up, an increase in GDP in the 1970s and the 1980s was caused by these unsustainable factors: a rapid increase in export, Reaganomics, and the bubble economy. In this sense, these factors were responsible for the 3–5% growth achieved during the period.

The rate of economic growth after the oil crisis was not zero in statistical figures. This led economists to be critical of Shimomura's zero-growth vision. However, if we exclude these special reasons, the rate of growth was essentially "zero" in Shimomura's sense—1–2%. In the 1990s, factors to boost the Japanese economy were absent, and the growth rate was around 1% per annum. In fact, in the first half of the 1990s, the government expanded public expenditure considerably to cope with the recession due to the bursting of the bubble economy.

The zero growth vision was incomprehensible to Japanese people. Firms and the government continued to invest, which caused excess capacity in many industries and a massive accumulation of bad loans in banks and debt in the government budget.

4.7 Zero Growth in the First Half of the 1990s

Dr. Shimomura passed away in 1989 when the bubble economy was at the final stage of a frivolous boom. We will examine what has happened since then.

Japanese economy slowed dramatically in the early 1990s when the bubble economy collapsed in 1990. This period was referred to as "lost decades," according to popular expression in journalism. The rate of growth was 1.4% per annum from 1991 to 1995 (see Table 3.2).

In 1989, the Bank of Japan raised the official discount rate from 2.5 to 3.25% to tighten the money market. The bursting of bubble caused a huge capital loss in construction, real estate industries, and financial institutions. As prices of stock and land dropped largely, a capital stock adjustment was needed in households and firms. They began to control expenditure.

From 1991 to 1995, private investment decreased 2.4% per annum and housing investment decreased 2.3% per annum. The government implemented an expansionary policy for economic recovery and large-scale measures centering on public investment. Public investment showed a big increase of 7.5% per annum. Unlike

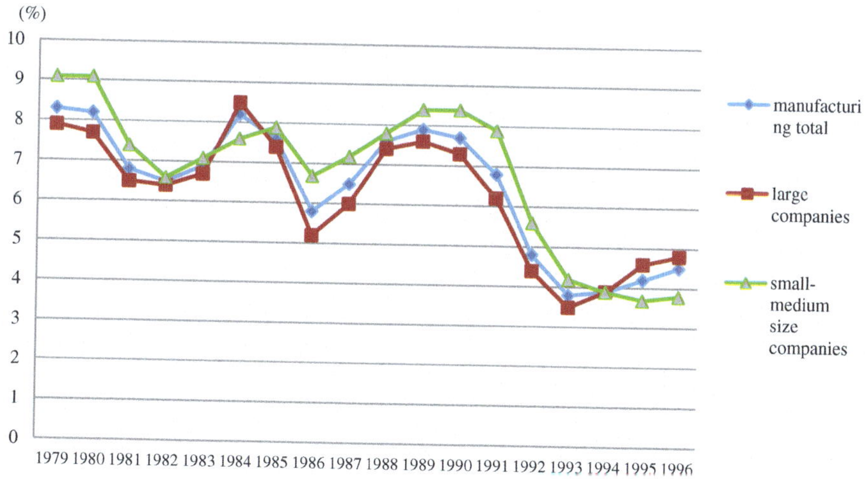

Fig. 4.3 Ratio of business income to total assets. *Note* (1) Business income = operating income + interest and dividends received. (2) Capital classification: large corporation is more than ¥1 billion, small-medium corporation is more than ¥10 million and less than ¥1 billion. *Source* Ministry of Finance "Quarterly Statistics of Corporate Firms"

the high growth period, the spillover effect of public investment was limited. As a consequence, the public sector balance as a share of nominal GDP changed from a surplus of 3.9% in 1990 to a deficit of 2.3% in 1995 (see Table 4.3). The government's fiscal balance deteriorated and the government had to issue deficit-financing bonds in 1994. There was an increase in construction bonds to finance public expenditure. In sum, the government lost fiscal discipline.

Due to appreciation of the yen and a protracted recession, the Japanese economy became deflationary and the rate of increase in nominal GDP was lower than that of real GDP.

1. Unstable foreign exchange rate

The yen rate to a dollar appreciated sharply. It was 145 yen in 1990 and went up to 94 yen in 1995. The yen rate remained in a serious misalignment. The appreciation of yen had a large impact on Japanese industries. The yen rate of 94 yen in 1995 was extremely high and exceeded the 101 yen of Purchasing Power Parity of machinery industry, which was the most competitive in all the industries in Japan (see Fig. 4.2). Due to economic depression and the appreciation of the yen, the rate of profit of firms declined considerably (see Fig. 4.3).[6] Owing to an appreciation of yen since the mid-1980s, the FDI of Japanese firms increased to the US and Asian countries. This tendency was fixed more clearly in 1990s, which, in turn, led to an increase in

[6]The rate of profit is the ratio of business income to total asset.

Japanese imports. Wide fluctuation and persistent misalignment of exchange rates changed employment levels, industrial structure, and corporate strategy.

Unstable exchange rate disturbs practices that contribute to steady management of real economy. If the exchange rate is stable, then an increase in labor productivity would be reflected either in an increase of wages in a growing economy or in a decrease of working hours in a zero-growth economy. The practice of keeping the unit labor costs constant was established during the period of high growth and fixed exchange rate system. The productivity-wage relationship contributed toward stabilizing the prices.

Dr. Shimomura asserted that it was not productive to discuss which exchange rate system was better, flexible rate or fixed rate. If each country in the world maintains internal and external equilibrium, then consequently the exchange rates would be stable. The most important rule of the game is that a national economy must maintain discipline.

4.8 Concluding Remarks

The oil shock in October 1973 had severe impacts on world economy, including Japan. Soon after the oil crisis, in January 1974, Dr. Shimomura published a paper in which he clearly expressed his vision of "zero growth" (1–2% a year) for the Japanese economy. Unfortunately, the politicians, business leaders, and economists did not accept his vision. However, the business continued as usual.

In order to stabilize zero growth, Dr. Shimomura emphasized the need for consumers, labor unions, businesses, banks, and the government to exercise "discipline." He urged us to change the pattern of behavior and the way of thinking of the high growth period. However, there was almost no change. Dr. Shimomura's discipline was not observed because people in the Japanese economy did not anticipate a zero-growth economy. As a result, today the Japanese economy is still in a state of disequilibrium. In particular, government debt has accumulated enormously. Discipline, instead of *laissez-faire*, should be a code of conduct in a zero-growth economy.

In the 1980s, Shimomura criticized Reaganomics and Japanese policy sharply. He also warned of an outbreak of the bubble economy. Dr. Shimomura's economic theory is based on the belief that each country should maintain a disciplinary policy for establishing a stable and sustainable national economy.

Dr. Shimomura was in favor voluntary export restraints (VERs) and opposed voluntary import expansions (VIEs). He was in favor of free trade when the postwar economic system of IMF and GATT worked effectively. However, he opposed free trade in a zero-growth economy. This shows another example of his discipline. It is understood that his economics is based on political economy, which aims at maintaining stability in the national economy. Stability in foreign exchange rate can be attained if each national economy maintains stability.

He also insisted that the international coordination of macroeconomic policy must be based on a principle that each country should make efforts to prioritize the formulation of disciplined domestic policies. In fact, Japan was compelled by the US to increase public investment and domestic-demand. Many politicians, economists, and journalists expressed that a policy focused on increasing domestic demand would contribute toward international coordination and that Japan should cooperate. Contrarily, Dr. Shimomura said, "Reaganomics of the US government is responsible for twin deficits. Japan is not to be blamed."

Dr. Shimomura warned that under zero-growth economy, growth-oriented policies such as an increase in public investment would not be effective and would lead to a government budget deficit. Industrial policy based on neo-liberalism, such as tax reforms (tax reduction on corporate profit and higher personal income), deregulation, and privatization, would neither activate the Japanese economy as a whole nor contribute toward decreasing the government budget deficit.

Dr. Shimomura firmly believed that economic growth would not be possible to attain simply by tax cuts. Economic growth reflects willingness and enthusiasm of a nation.

In summing up, the increase in GDP in the 1970s and the 1980s was caused by these unsustainable factors: a rapid increase in export, Reaganomics, and the bubble economy. In this sense, without them it was clear that 3–5% growth would not be realized.

The rate of economic growth after the oil crisis was not zero in statistical figures. This caused economists to be critical of Shimomura's zero-growth vision. However, if we exclude these special reasons, the rate of growth was essentially "zero" in Dr. Shimomura's sense—1–2%. In the 1990s, factors to boost the Japanese economy were absent, and the growth rate was around 1% per annum.

In the 1990s, global environmental problems, such as global warming and loss of rainforest, worsened further. Therefore, sustainability, instead of growth, has become the main agenda for both advanced and developing countries. In order to restrict our economic activities within natural material cycle, our economy will have to be controlled within the upper limit of usable oil and fossil energy. There will be a limit to our economic activities. In this sense, we have to consider seriously Dr. Shimomura's vision of zero-growth.

Dr. Shimomura had a sharp macroeconomic intuition, which formed the basis for his bold vision. An accurate vision is important for politicians, business leaders, and economists.

References

Horiuchi, K. (1998). *Vision and policy of the Japanese economy: From growth to development*. Tokyo: Toyo Keizai Press. (in Japanese).

Horiuchi, K. (2007). *Dr. Shimomura and the Japanese economy*. Tokyo: Development Bank of Japan, Research Institute of Capital Formation. (in Japanese).

Horiuchi, K. (2014). Vision of the Japanese economy and social common capital. In Y. Mamiya, K. Horiuchi, & K. Uchiyama (Eds.), *The Japanese economy: Social common capital and sustainable development*. Tokyo: University of Tokyo Press. (in Japanese).
Shimomura, O. (1974). Japanese economy is on a zero-growth track. *Economist, 52*(2), 10–15. (in Japanese).
Shimomura, O. (1976). Japanese economy: Challenges and future choices. In Japan Development Bank (Ed.), *Choices for tomorrow: in commemoration of the 25th anniversary of the Japan Development Bank*. Tokyo: JDB (in Japanese).
Shimomura, O. (1981). *Discipline and the Japanese economy*. Tokyo: Toyo keizai Press. (in Japanese).
Shimomura, O. (1987a). Zaitech will destroy enterprise. *Bungei Shunju, 65*(2), 112–120. (in Japanese).
Shimomura, O. (1987b). *Japan is not to blame. NESCO*. Tokyo: Bungei Shunju (in Japanese).
Shimomura, O., & Suzuki, Y. (1978). *Economic policies in low-growth period*. Tokyo: Toyo Keizai Press. (in Japanese).

Part II
Implications of Zero Growth Vision: Lost Decades, Sustainability, and Corporate Management

Chapter 5
Current Zero Growth Era

Abstract This chapter considers what the economic factors make that contributed towards stagnation in the Japanese economy so stagnant. We focus on the following three factors: surge in foreign direct investment (FDI); enlarged aggregate demand management policies, and; serious digression of managerial skills. First, the flux of FDI deprives Japanese workers of good employment opportunities, and causes a decline in domestic capital investment, thereby, extinguishing opportunities of business upturn. Second, public-debt accumulation is accelerated around the turn of the twenty first century. Unless the government goes to bankrupt, the current expansionary fiscal-monetary policies is unsustainable. This fact implies that the "Growth Strategy" has a numbering effect, and Japan would witness the economic devastation unless the inefficiency in the supply side of the economy were improved. Finally, the Japanese social security system depends on the overall growth of the economy. There is likelihood that the rapid aging and reduction of population would possibly topple the system from the bottom. This scenario would require needs heightening the production efficiency urgently. We provide a mathematical example in which the progress in managerial skills emerges on an immediately basic urgency as a change in the total factor productivity (TFP). The results show that observed lower or negative growth TFP suggesting stagnation or deterioration in managerial-skill development.

Keywords Foreign direct investment · Industrial hollowing · Efficient information processing · Fiscal crisis · Aging · Population decline · Total factor productivity

5.1 Introduction

This chapter considers reasons behind the long stagnation, if we can call it that, why the Japanese economy experiences such a long economic stagnation. Moreover, we explore whether there remains the potentiality of boosting economic growth in the Japanese economy. It must be noted that a zero-growth economy is not necessarily

K. Horiuchi and M. Otaki, *Dr. Osamu Shimomura's Legacy and the Postwar Japanese Economy*, Development Bank of Japan Research Series,
DOI 10.1007/978-981-10-5762-5_5

gloomy. As will be discussed in Chap. 6, a stationary state, which is included in the concept of the zero growth, can be a vivid economy, in which new and efficient industries emerge while old and inefficient industries are thwarted. Essentially, even though the scale of the economy is not enlarged and GDP is presumably kept constant, the economy can be entirely renovated and made more efficient. This type of stationary economy is highly desirable, when we deeply think of the ultimate economic constraint (i.e., scarcity of natural resources). When Shimomura advocated his zero-growth scheme, the bottleneck of production resource was crude oil.[1] In contrast to oil in Shimomura's days, less carbon in atmosphere poses a problem owing to the global warming problem. We regard the current Japanese economy as being located in this transition process towards a stationary state. That is, economic growth is not imperative.

In this chapter, as a preparation for Chap. 6, we analyze the reasons that make the Japanese economy unfavorable to prompt economic growth. Among economic factors, which inevitably lead to zero growth in the Japanese economy, we concentrate on the following three factors: globalization; limit of the aggregate demand management policies; demographic factor.

First, globalization, in particular, affects the structure of the Japanese firms driven by the deregulation of the labor market. To put it simply, de facto, the firing rights of firm is quite strengthened. This causes the flux of foreign direct investment (FDI). This is attributed to the fact that, instead of firing high-wage Japanese workers, it is advantageous for the Japanese firms, to move their domestic factories and affiliates and hiring cheaper labor forces in the East Asia. Thus, FDI narrows the domestic capital investment and the opportunities of employment. This deprives the aggregate demand, which results in the structural stagnation.

Second, with the outbreak of the bubble economy, since the early 1990s, Japan has been suffering to record a huge amount of fiscal deficit. The sum of public debt is around 1300 trillion yen in 2016, which soars up to 2.5 times as large as its GDP. Consequently, in conjunction with the aging problem, Japan suffers from a quite stuckicks to its fiscal crisis in reality. Despite the crisis scenario, the government has stuck to expansionary fiscal-monetary policy to maintain ephemeral prosperity. Taking into consideration in Japan's brief history from the beginning of this century, it would be evident that expansionary policy is not a suitable remedy for the Japanese economy. Such policy is quite precarious in the sense that it might trigger a default of public debts and/or hyperinflation. The aggregate demand management policies have numbering effect. The supply-side of the economy, and not the demand side, is attributed to the cause, which makes the Japanese economy

[1]It must be noted that Shimomura's zero-growth was defined more widely given. He regarded zero-growth as a slightly positive economic growth around 1–2%. This rate corresponds to the actual average growth rate of Japan since the outbreak bust of the bubble at the beginning of the 1990s. In this sense, Shimomura's prediction was correct although he could not ascertain this fact (Shimomura passed away at 1989). However, unexpected depressive socio-economic factors, which are analyzed in this chapter, emerge from the 1990s, the zero growth in Shimomura's sense becomes unsustainable.

the inefficiency. An organization such as firm exists because there are many opportunities that an organization can solve economic problems more efficiently than market. These organizations are equipped with information that the markets do not possess. Information processing plays a crucial role. Idealistically, information, which market provides, is limited to price. Contrary, much information is processed within a firm such as characteristics and needs of customers and feasibility of various projects. Efficient information processing depends on sincerity and conscience. Whenever fraud and incompetence prevail, an organization becomes dysfunctional. In such a scenario executives and/or employees are driven by myopic self-interests, processed information contains much of noise and is biased. Subsequently decisions, as an entity, are rendered unsuitable for meeting the needs of the situation. This has been causing the melt-down of Japanese firms since the beginning of the century.[2] This is closely related to the deregulation of labor market as mentioned earlier. To summarize, the Japanese firm becomes reluctant to invest in human capital intensively. It would not be possible for Japan to find new and promising industries, which is vital for establishing an economy in stationary state.[3]

Finally, we discuss the problem of an aging and large population reducing problem in Japan from the view of macroeconomic theory. It is a plausible first order approximation to measure the affluence of a country by its GDP *per capita*. Since the population of Japan is estimated to reduce from 130 billion to 90 billion by 2050, it is likely that the current GDP will fall about 30% to the extent that we assume that the GDP *per capita* is kept invariant. This fact implies that negative growth throughout the transition process does not lead to the impoverishment of Japanese citizens. In this sense, the emphasis on adopting and the implementing "Growth Strategy" (Seicho Senryaku) by the current cabinet is arguable.

Nevertheless, it must be noted that there are some important economic institutes that presume a significantly positive economic growth rate. One such institution is the public annuity fund, which is based on pay-as-you-go system. It is evident that the issue of a rapidly aging population has fatally damaged the public annuity fund. Hence it is unavoidable that an alternative annuity system, which mainly depends on the income transfer within the same generation, is desirable. This system would not only be immune from the reduction of population, but would also contribute towards equalizing income distribution. The other problematic institute is the

[2]In Chap. 6, we reconsider the corporate governance problem from a different perspective.

[3]Many light-headed economists dubs the era from the 1990s to the 2000s "The Lost Two Decades." Their ritual phrase is "Regulation delays the economic recovery. More deregulation!" Elementary economics teaches us that entirely laissez-faire economy achieves the best consequence only under quite an idealistic situation (The first-fundamental theory of welfare economics) such as perfect competition and perfect information. In general, such presumptions are not upheld. Accordingly, even though we must prioritize free economic behavior, simultaneously, we must accept the corresponding regulation to achieve the best outcomes. In this sense, the flux of deregulation is evidently unwise. The Japanese economy needs the rational and liberal economic thoughts and discussions based on the economic reality.

medical care system. The system prioritizes senior citizens far more than young generations, although the burden on medical care is attributed to them. This is a typical example of intergenerational inequality, which is also related to the huge accumulation of public debt. It is our serious concern that whether Japanese can define an ethic of what life is.

However, there is no denying that Japan has to heighten the labor productivity. This problem also has the roots within the inefficiency of the supply-side structure as aforementioned. While autonomous productivity growth is often measured by changes in TFP, what comprises TFP is quite obscure. This is because TFP is defined by the measurement error of production function. To the extent that TFP analysis is considered to be meaningful, there should be vital production resources, which are intangible. Efficient information processing is one of the most important managerial skills as discussed above. This efficiency prompts the coordination of workers. The need for such coordination originates from the inseparability of jobs. We regard efficiency of information processing as the progress in corporative behavior and show that the progress in efficiency can appear as the TFP of the aggregate production function. Lesser growth in the TFP reveals limitation of the managerial skills.

5.2 Effects of Globalization

5.2.1 Labor Market Deregulation

Labor market deregulation began at 1996 just before the Asia Financial Crisis. By 2003, the gist of the revised Worker Dispatching Law (Rodosha Haken Ho) and Employment Security Law (Shokugyo Antei Ho) had been settled.[4] The scheme of the deregulation is to facilitate the mass entry of dispatched workers into a firm. Since there is area serious wage gaps between tenured employee and dispatched worker, which amounts to 2 million yen (40 age; male; Basic Survey on Wage Structure; Ministry of Health, Employment and Welfare) as in Figs. 5.1 and 5.2, every firm prefers to employ dispatched workers.

The existence of abundant cheap labor force in East Asia at which makes such a cruel disparity possible is the very existence of incomparable cheap labor. That is a kind of arbitration of wages between different economies. It must be noted that, as illustrated by Fig. 5.3 (Development Bank of Japan), a surge of FDI coincides with the deregulation of the labor market (the vertical axe is the ratio of FDI to domestic capital investment in the manufacturing industry).

[4]See Yanagisawa (2008) for precise analysis of this process. Otaki (2015a, pp. 96–97) finds that the income disparity between employee and employer remarkably is enlarged from the turn of the twenty first century.

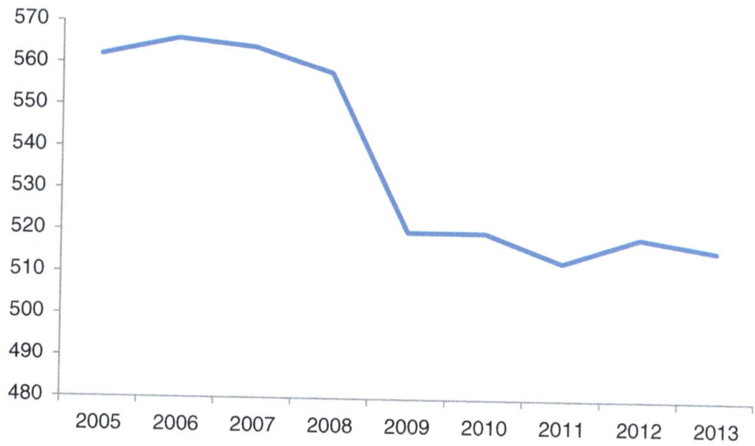

Fig. 5.1 Normal wage (ten thousand yen: regular worker)

Fig. 5.2 Nominal wage (ten thousand yen: dispatched worker)

5.2.2 *Surge in Foreign Direct Investment: Economic Hollowing*

In this subsection, we analyze how the surge of FDI affects the Japanese economy. As discussed in the previous subsection, the deregulation of the labor market stimulates FDI towards East Asia. We here consider its economic consequences. First, the change in the domestic capital investment is examined. According to the Basic Survey of Overseas Business Activities (BSOBA; Ministry of Economy,

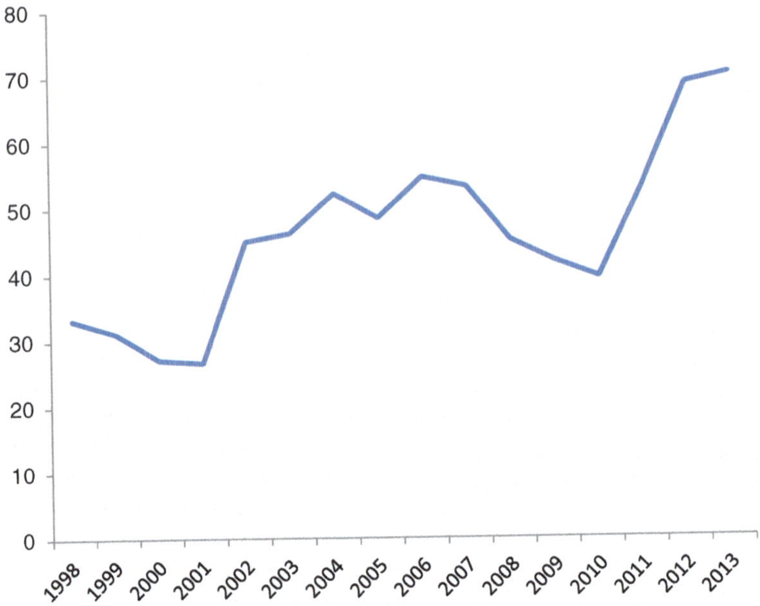

Fig. 5.3 The outflow of FDI in Japan (Manufacturing industry)

Trade and Industry: Kaigai Jigyo Katsudo Kihon Chosa), the ratio of overseas capital investment to the domestic investment is about 20% in 2005 and 30% in 2014.[5] SNA reveals that the sum of the domestic capital investment amounted to 70 trillion yen at 2005, and the same level is kept at 2014. When we regard the sample corporations in BSOBA possess the same properties as that in SNA. We find that the following investment opportunities diverted overseas:

$$70 \times 0.2 = 14 \text{ trillion yen during 2005,} \tag{5.1}$$

$$70 \times 0.3 = 21 \text{ trillion yen during 2014.} \tag{5.2}$$

Essentially, a substantial amount of the aggregate investment was diverted overseas.[6] It is certain that such a large void in the home economy thwarts the expansionary effect of aggregate demand management policies.[7] This is because the

[5]It must be noted that these figures include non-manufacturing industries.

[6]One might argue that cumulative investment costs are sunk in overseas factories and affiliates, and hence, intensive FDI behavior is the rational response of Japanese firms. However, as will be discussed below, when we recognize JPY is not the key currency under a flexible exchange rate system, it is arguable whether investment costs are really sunk and repayable.

[7]See Otaki (2015b, Chap. 13) for more detail on the income effect to capital investment in a general equilibrium growth model. This income effect is verified only when the good markets are engaged in monopolistic competition.

second effect of the multiplier is weakened: a business upturn also leads entrepreneurs to optimistic future expectations, and further stimulates domestic capital investment. This is a virtuous cycle. However, FDI annihilates such a cycle. These depressive effects depicting as the leakage of employment opportunities and/or decrease in the domestic capital investment are referred to *economic hollowing*.

Second, it is arguable whether FDI produces substantial benefits. It is well known that the U.K. (pre-World war II) and the US (current) are the most intensive FDI countries. However, one must note that each country was (is) the key currency country on the corresponding era. They are almost free from the exchange rate risk. In contrast, Japan is exposed to the volatile fluctuations of the exchange rate. Roughly speaking, Japanese FDI earns money in terms of the US dollar (USD). If firms remit their earnings to the home country, they must sell USD and purchase Japanese yen (JPY). Accordingly, JPY appreciates against USD. This implies that some part of the remitted earnings disappear when they are evaluated in terms of JPY.

Thus, FDI does not earn substantial benefits enough as it looks. According to BSOBA (2014), the average profit ratio of overseas manufacturing affiliates against total sales is around 4.7% (2007–2014). The Financial Statements Statistics of Corporations by Industry (FSSCI: Ministry of Finance) reveals that that ratio in the domestic manufacturing industry is around 4.1% (2007–2014). Although the average profit ratio of the overseas affiliate seems to be higher than that of the domestic manufacturing industry, the effect of the change in the nominal exchange rate during the corresponding periods must be considered. The nominal exchange rate appreciates about 10% (1.4% per annum Bank of Japan). If all overseas profits are earned in terms of USD, the approximate profit rate of overseas affiliate in terms of JPY is

$$4.7 - 1.4 = 3.3(\%).$$

This figure indicates that there are hardly any economic motives to remit earned overseas profits to Japan except for needs for accounting of the parent company. There is no denying that the retained profit ratio against the net profit in overseas manufacturing industry is far higher than in that in the home country (Iwase and Sato (2014), BSOBA (2014)). This is one of the indirect but persuasive evidence, which suggests that the appreciation JPY hinders the remittance of overseas Japanese affiliates.[8] We define the phenomenon that the anxiety about the appreciation of the nominal exchange rate hinders the remittance of earnings from FDI is as the *rock-in effect to remittance*.

To summarize this subsection, deregulation in the labor market triggered the flux of FDI. FDI not merely causes economic hollowing but also the rock-in effect to remittance. Consequently, the spurious cost reduction, which emerges from

[8]According to BSOBA (2014), the net profits of overseas Japanese affiliate amounts to 7 trillion JPY. FSSCI (2014) estimates that such profit of the domestic corporation is about 37 trillion JPY. 16% of profits are emerged from overseas. Hence, no one can neglect the economic consequences of FDI whenever one explores the future of the Japanese economy.

employing cheap labor force available in East Asia, is rather harmful than beneficial against the initial intention of labor market deregulation. The fluctuation of the nominal exchange rate segregates a company into almost unrelated overseas affiliates. Even though the name of a company is the same, each of division is identified as a different company. If the capital investment cost is sunk, at least privately, and the initial decision is hardly reversible, then emigration towards East Asia would be the only medium of benefiting from the overseas earnings. Nevertheless, this procedure should be strictly prohibited to avoid unnecessary political strains. Eventually, unless FDI is reconsidered from the view point of collective decision, an important part of Japan's growth potential will be deprived forever.

5.3 Limit of Aggregate Demand Management Policy

5.3.1 Dissolved Organic Growth Mechanism: Inefficiency in Management Is the Acute Cause of Stagnant Growth

As discussed in Introduction, the annihilation of efficient information processing is quite a serious problem in Japan. Although this subsection considers the limits to the effectiveness of the aggregate demand management policy, capital investment is considered the node of the demand and supply side decision. On the one hand, capital investment consists of the aggregate demand. On the other hand, capital investment extends the production capacity. Therefore, it is meaningful to know how the inefficiency of supply-side decision deteriorates the aggregate demand management policy.

In the previous subsection, we considered the inefficiency of FDI caused by the lack of wise collective decision. Inefficiency of FDI belongs to a kind of *fallacy of composition*. When only one firm invests overseas, it can enjoy the benefits of a cheap labor force and the lock-in effect does not occur because its remittance is very small, relatively to the scale of the foreign exchange market. However, numerous firms invest overseas. If all of them remit their earnings, then the nominal exchange rate appreciates (i.e., the lock-in effect to remittance would emerge). Thus, an economic consequence, which can be applied to single firm's behavior, is not upheld in the case of an industry as a whole. Accordingly, the surge of FDI is a typical example of fallacy of composition.[9] The only solution for a fallacy of composition is the wise collective decision. An economy-wide adjustment of the schedule of FDI was acutely desirable to avoid the excess FDI. The government should have been moderator of various industries. One of the most important causes that led to the realization of achieved the High-growth era is the efficient and dense communication between the public and private sector. Thus, excessive FDI

[9]See Otaki (2015b, Chap. 9) for more rigorous discussion on this problem.

exemplifies that efficient information processing is annihilated even at the top management in the current Japanese economy.

Such mismanagement, owing to inefficient information processing for wise collective decision, is not confined to FDI, and evident through decisions of firm as an entity. In general, a corporation comprises an organic entity. That is, there is a prominent *inseparability* between the jobs in a corporation. Inseparability can be regarded as the positive externality of one workers' ethic to other workers'. In reality, the boundary of job to job blurs. Accordingly, one's work ethic is contagious to others'. When a worker is diligent enough to take the effect that his devotion heightens other's productivity into consideration, a more efficient production process is established. We dub these externalities among workers as *inseparability of jobs*.

Explicit job descriptions neglect the existence of such inseparability and prevent the internalization of these positive externalities. Thus, the norm of payment according to ability proves to be hazardous for the overall productivity of a firm. This is because such a payment system can hardly evaluate the indirect contribution of a worker in easing tasks of other workers. One must note that Coase's (1937) assertion that an organization emerges instead of the market because the former can solve economic problems, which the latter cannot. Inseparability of a production resource is a typical example of this assertion.[10]

To illustrate how the inseparability of jobs works within a firm, we construct a simple model below. We assume that this representative firm comprises two individual employees. The game is a two-stage game. At the first stage, both players decide their effort level, e_i, and the total outcome is determined. The second stage negotiates their payoffs in accordance to the Nash bargaining solution. Let the total outcome be denoted as y, and the increase function of the efficiency unit of labor, L_i. L_i is the increase function of each player's effort, e_i. That is,

$$\begin{aligned} y &= \psi(L_1, L_2, y^d) - \psi(L_2, L_1, y^d), \\ L_1 &= L(e_1, L_2), L_2 = L(e_2, L_1), \end{aligned} \tag{5.3}$$

where y^d is the parameter that represents the level of the aggregate demand. The reason why the aggregated demand enters into the production function implies that production opportunities increase along with the aggregate demand. That is, our theory implicitly assumes that some frictions exist in the matching between sellers and purchasers. Additionally, whenever purchasing activity becomes more intensive, a producer encounters a customer with a higher probability. Both players feel disutility increasing with their effort level. Let the disutility function, G, be defined as follows:

$$G_i = G(e_i), G' > 0, G'' > 0. \tag{5.4}$$

[10]Otaki (2015a, Chap. 5) considers the reason *d'être* of a firm from the perspective of nurturing dexterity.

Since it costs workers to establish deep mutual understandings, the G function contains these intangible costs.

This two-stage game must be solved by backward induction. One must note that the game is symmetric, and hence, the equilibrium strategies become identical. Since the individuals have already delivered their work in the first stage, the threat point of Nash bargaining solution is $(G(e_1), G(e_2))$. The corresponding Nash product, $\Pi(w)$, is

$$\Pi(w) = [y - w - G(e_1)] \cdot [w - G(e_2)], \tag{5.5}$$

where w is the real wage, which an employee receives. The solution of the second stage is

$$(w_1, w_2) = \left(\frac{y - G(e_1) - G(e_2)}{2}, \frac{y - G(e_1) - G(e_2)}{2}\right). \tag{5.6}$$

Thus, the payoff function, $P(e_1, e_2)$, of the first-stage game is identical between employees. That is,

$$P(e_1, e_2) \equiv \frac{y - G(e_1) - G(e_2)}{2}. \tag{5.7}$$

In the following, we classify the resource allocation in accordance to the type of equilibrium.

(i) The Case for Nash Equilibrium

In this case, both players regard the counterpart's effort as given. The maximization condition leads us to the following reaction curve:

$$\frac{\partial \psi}{\partial L_1} \cdot \frac{\partial L_1}{\partial e_1} = G'(e_1). \tag{5.8}$$

Differentiating both sides of Eq. (5.8), we obtain

$$\begin{aligned} &\left[\frac{\partial^2 \psi}{\partial L_1^2} \cdot \frac{\partial L_1}{\partial e_1} + \frac{\partial \psi}{\partial L_1} \cdot \frac{\partial^2 L_1}{\partial e_1^2}\right] de_1 + \left[\left[\frac{\partial \psi}{\partial L_1}\right]^2 \cdot \frac{\partial L_1}{\partial e_1} + \frac{\partial \psi}{\partial L_1} \cdot \frac{\partial^2 L_1}{\partial e_1 \partial e_2}\right] de_2 \\ &\qquad + \left[\frac{\partial^2 \psi}{\partial L_1 \partial y} \cdot \frac{\partial L_1}{\partial e_1} + \frac{\partial \psi}{\partial L_1} \cdot \frac{\partial^2 L_1}{\partial e_1 \partial y}\right] \cdot dy^d \\ &\qquad = G''(e_1) de_1 \\ &\qquad \Rightarrow \frac{de_1}{de_2} > 0. \end{aligned} \tag{5.9}$$

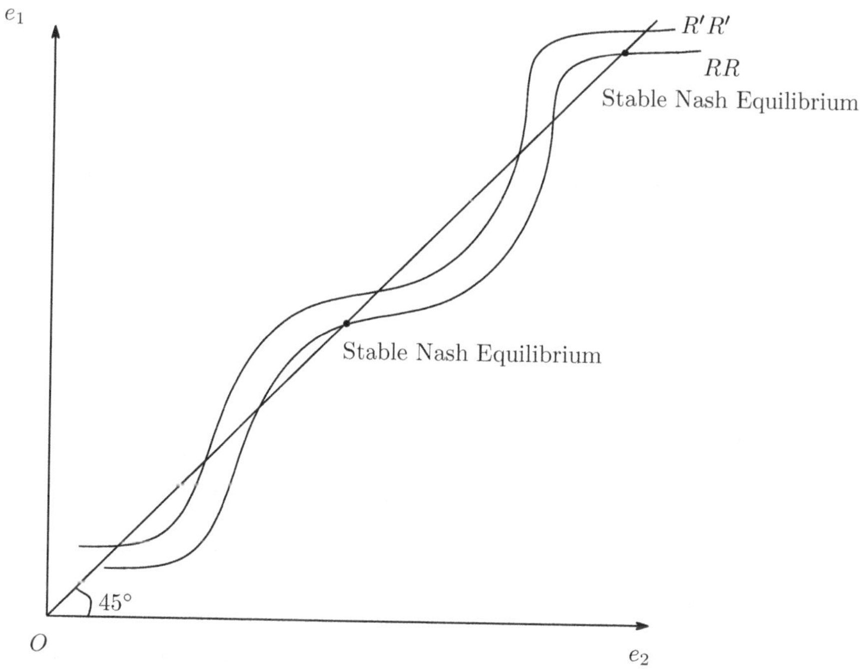

Fig. 5.4 The reaction curve

Accordingly, the reaction curve is upward sloping. Since the equilibrium is symmetric, as illustrated in Fig. 5.4, each Nash equilibrium corresponds to an intersection of the reaction curve *RR* and the 45 degree line. There are possibly multiple equilibria. This is because the game possesses the strategic compliment property when an employee possesses a higher work ethic, this also contributes to heightening the productivity of his counterpart, and thus this counterpart also becomes in higher work ethic. If the personal evaluation is done properly and he receives a financial incentive in accordance to his true effort, it would enhance the workers' discipline. As such, Pareto-ranked Nash equilibria can coexist. Meanwhile, if the aggregate demand, y^d, increases, when the marginal productivity of labor, $\frac{\partial\psi}{\partial l_d}$, and the marginal increase of the efficiency unit of labor, $\frac{\partial l_1}{\partial e_1}$, is an increasing function of the aggregate demand, an elementary calculus finds that the reaction curve shifts upward as Curve $R'R'$. This comes from the fact that an upturn in the aggregate demand extends the exchange opportunities of goods and wasted production is reduced.

(ii) The Case for Rational Collective Decision

However, even the best outcome achieved by Nash equilibrium is second best. This is because both players do not count their own in relation to other. In other words, while the boundary between management and work blurs due to the inseparability of jobs, the concept of Nash equilibrium implies that both players behave as though there is a clear line between jobs. An optimal allocation can be achieved only through the collective decision-making, not through the decentralized decision system such as the Nash equilibrium.

The desirable collective decision is as follows. First, one must solve the downside equation in (5.3) on (L_1, L_2), which induces the following equations:

$$dL_i = \frac{1}{1-\left[\frac{\partial L_1}{\partial e_2}\right]^2}\cdot\left[\frac{\partial L_1}{\partial e_1}de_i + \frac{\partial L_1}{\partial e_1}\frac{\partial L_1}{\partial e_2}de_j\right] \Leftrightarrow L_i = \lambda(e_i, e_j). \tag{5.10}$$

The numerator of Eq. (5.10) depicts how each individual contributes to raise the efficiency unit of one's labor. The first term represent the direct effect, which comes from an individual's efforts. The second term is the indirect effect, which emerges from his partner's strife. This positive externality stems from the inseparability of jobs. The term, $\frac{1}{1-\left[\frac{\partial L_1}{\partial e_2}\right]^2}$, depicts the cumulative effect or multiplier effect (if we may call it that). This effect implies that there is a virtuous cycle in heightening work ethic—if an individual becomes more diligent, this makes the job of his counterpart easier and more interesting, and thus, the associate heightens his work ethic. The effect of one laborer reflects to him, who strives much more, this leads a virtuous cycle. To summarize, an increase in effort extends the efficiency unit of labor.

Maximizing Eq. (5.7) with respect to (e_1, e_2) with taking into consideration the relationship in Eq. (5.10), one obtains

$$\left[\frac{\partial \psi}{\partial L_1}\cdot\frac{\partial L_1}{\partial e_1} + \frac{\partial \psi}{\partial L_1}\cdot\frac{\partial L_1}{\partial e_2}\right] = G'(e_1). \tag{5.11}$$

Comparing Eqs. (5.11) with (5.8), one finds that the second term of the right-hand side of Eq. (5.11) is added. This positive term represents an *encouraging effect*, which means that the counterpart is encouraged by the help of his diligent coworker to overlap fields. Such overlapping fields exist owing to the inseparability of jobs. It is evident that for a given aggregate demand level, y^d, equilibrium effort level, $e^*(y^d)$, is always larger than that in all possible Nash equilibrium, $e^N(y^d)$. This property of the model suggests that collective decision is unavoidable whenever there is inseparability of jobs. This property can be regarded as a mathematical foundation for the existence of a firm, which is advocated by Coase (1937).

In addition, this discussion implies that the supply curve under the optimal collective decision is located at the most leftward position; it is labeled as Curve SS^*

Fig. 5.5 The supply curve

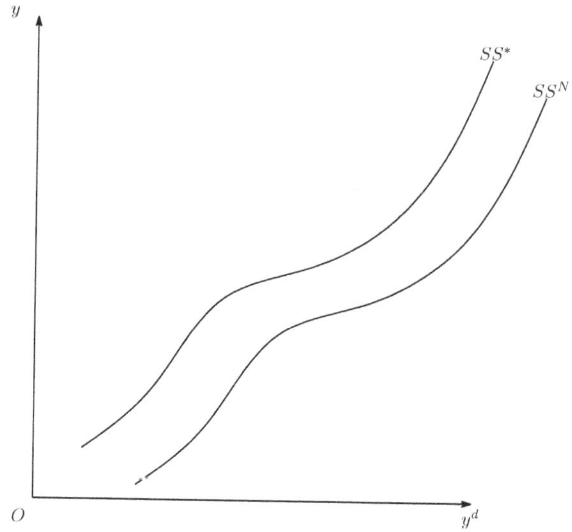

in Fig. 5.5.[11] Other possible supply curve achieved by Nash equilibrium is, for example, Curve SS^N.[12]

Given the state of the aggregate demand, y^d, and the insufficient coordination between employees, the production level of a firm, y, reduces further. In other words, such reduction of productivity caused by a dissociating coordination culture within a firm is cumulatively thwarted through the discouraging effect due to the decomposition of jobs that are intrinsically inseparable. When the coordination culture degenerates more rapidly than the expansionary aggregate demand management policy, the economy fails to gain substantial benefit from such a policy. This only results in leaving a tax burden for the future generation.[13]

When the Nash equilibrium allocation is achieved, the real wage becomes equal to the private marginal product of effort [see Eq. (5.8)]. Accordingly, the real wage is sapped in conjunction with the progress in the irrational job demarcation. This is the other side of inefficient management. Thus, regarding firm as an organic entity that consists of inseparable jobs, the recent tendency in Japanese firms wherein workers focus only on their jobs and show little interest in their adjacent fields

[11]The aggregate supply function is mathematically defined as

$$y = \psi\left(\lambda\left(e^*\left(y^d\right), e^*\left(y^d\right)\right), \lambda\left(e^*\left(y^d\right), e^*\left(y^d\right)\right), y^d\right). \tag{5.12}$$

[12]Note that there is no guarantee that the aggregate supply curve is continuous when there are multiple Nash equilibria. This is because a bifurcation possibly occurs along with an increase in the aggregate demand (see Fig. 5.4). For the sake of simplicity, we exclude such a case. Even though the aggregate supply function is discontinuous, such a curve is located rightward of AS^*.

[13]Otaki (2015c) rigorously proves that there is no exception that the issuance of public debt becomes the burden of the future generation, which is measured by welfare term.

makes a firm dysfunctional. One must note that a firm, as described by the neoclassical linear homogenous production function, is not a firm in reality. This is because anyone can establish a firm that represents as the neoclassical philosophy type by gathering separable production resources in the market. A prominent tendency that firms can be easily merged and bought for improving profitability is seen in the "Structural Reformation" (Kozo Kaikaku) of the Koizumi cabinet.[14] However, whenever one evokes the seriousness of the inseparability of jobs, it is not deniable that such a tendency aggravates the performance of the overall firm. Coordination of workers who have been educated in different firms is not an easy task as it is considered. Moreover, as aforementioned, the difficulty of managing merged firms as an organic entity stems from the inseparability of jobs. Consequently, the aggregate supply for a given aggregate demand management policy possibly becomes curtailed. This acutely narrows the possibility of economic growth.

5.3.2 *Aggregate Demand Management as Opium*

In this subsection, we consider the effect of the aggregate demand management in relation a of firm's production. For simplicity, let the aggregate demand function be defined as

$$y^d \equiv cy + m, \quad 1 > c > 0, \tag{5.13}$$

where c is the marginal propensity to consume and m is the real cash balance, which is a policy variable in the theory.[15] Since the aggregate supply function can be written

$$y \equiv \theta\left(y^d\right), \quad 1 > c\theta' > 0, \tag{5.14}$$

from Eq. (5.12), one can illustrate the equilibrium condition of the goods market as in Fig. 5.6. When one substitutes Eqs. (5.14) into (5.13), one obtains the following quasi-reduced form of the aggregate demand function:

$$y^d = c\theta\left(y^d\right) + m. \tag{5.15}$$

---

[14]For more precise discussion on the Structural Reformation, see Otaki (2015a, Chaps. 5 and 6).

[15]This type of aggregate demand function is derived from two period overlapping-generations model with a linear homogenous Cobb-Douglas utility function. Equilibrium price can be determined independently from the nominal money supply. Concerning this subject, see Otaki (2015b, Chap. 2) for more detail.

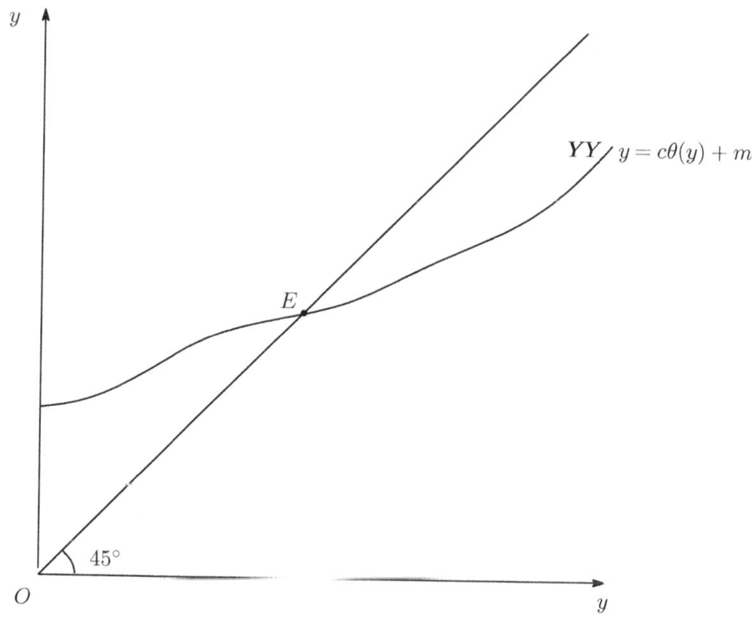

Fig. 5.6 Equilibrium of good market

Setting $y^d = y$ in equilibrium, and differentiating Eq. (5.15),

$$[1 - c\theta']dy = dm. \tag{5.16}$$

Thus the locus of Eq. (5.15) is Curve *YY* and it is upward sloping and the slope is located within $(0, 1)$. The intersection *E* of Curves *YY* and the 45 degree line is the equilibrium of the good market.[16]

Let the average productivity under the optimal collective decision and that under a Nash equilibrium be defined as θ^* and θ^N, respectively. As shown in the previous subsection, $\theta^* > \theta^N$ holds. Accordingly the corresponding reduced form aggregate demand functions become Curves YY^* and YY^N as illustrated in Fig. 5.7. The equilibrium is achieved when the economy is located at Point E^* when $\theta = \theta^*$ and Point E^N when $\theta = \theta^N$. Thus, the inefficiency due to mismanagement resulting from the excess decomposition of jobs makes the aggregate demand policy less effective. Moreover, this possibly provokes the negative growth rate. The reason is that the inefficiency reduces the aggregate income via lowering workers' effort and thwarts the aggregate demand. This movement is consistent with a curtailed production

[16] $y^d = \theta(y^d)$ may have many solutions. However, the solution, which possesses the economic meaning, is confined to the case, where Eq. (5.15) is upheld. That is, the solution should be limited to the case where $y^d = \frac{m}{1-c}$. Figure 5.6 confirms the existence of such a solution.

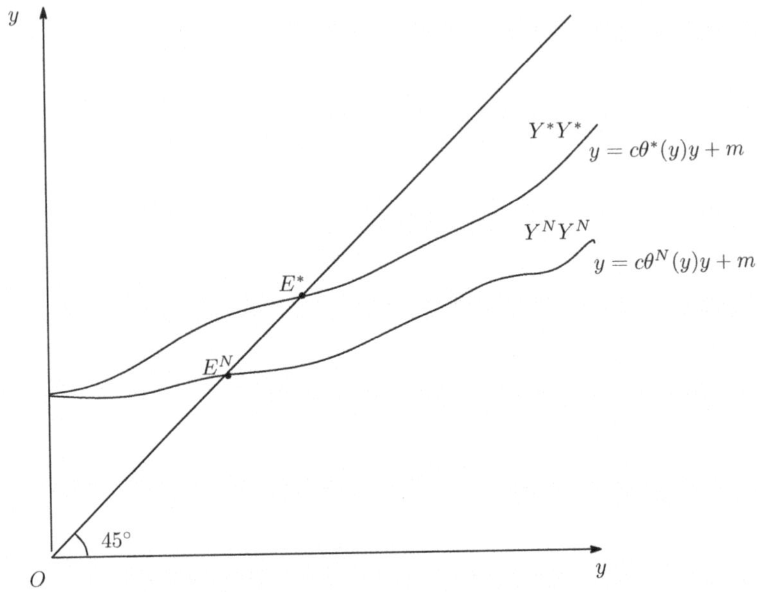

Fig. 5.7 Inefficiency of production process

level. The surge of FDI discussed in Sect. 5.3.1 is the very example of coordination failure.

To regain the vigor in the economy, which falls due to inefficient management, radical and expansionary aggregate demand policies are prompted. When the inefficient management prevails, the economy moves from Point E^* to E^N. An expansionary fiscal policy, which is financed by the issuance of the widely defined liquidity (i.e., issuance of new money or public bond), increases the real cash balance. Consequently, it is inevitable to lift the economy to Point E^* to boost the fiscal-monetary expenditure. We regard such situation as the current zero-growth era where the Japanese economy is entrapped.

For worse, the enforcement of expansionary aggregate management policy is far facile than heightening the efficiency of firms. This is because precise reexaminations to organic structure of overall industries are far more difficult than the decisions on the government expenditure. Moreover, since the substantial situation of the economy has remained unchanged except the accumulation of the widely defined liquidity, there is no incentive for firms to improve their systematic inefficiency. When the effect of expansionary policy would exceed the degree of the degeneration in firm's power as an organic entity, the economy might experiences a positive growth rate. In such a gloomy scenario, firms will misunderstand that the decomposition of jobs heightens efficiency, and this tendency might become a cumulative process:

Decomposition of jobs ⇒ Excessive fiscal policy ⇒ Positive economic growth
⇒ Decomposition of jobs ⇒ ⋯

Thus, the degeneration of firm as an organic entity is accelerated by expansionary fiscal-monetary policy, which is gradually enlarged by the requirement of economy to sustain a slightly positive growth. As such, the aggregate demand management policy is considered to have an opium-like existence in the sense that while this policy contributes to achieve a minor economic growth in the short run, a slowdown of productivity and rapid accumulation of public debt ensue, which ultimately bother the economy in the long run.

5.4 Our Theory and TFP Analysis: Reduction of Labor Force and Economic Growth

As mentioned in Introduction, population reduction due to aging poses a serious problem for Japan. Accordingly, small numbers of work force or tax payers are obliged to support the large retired generation. The public pension funds and medical care system are built on the assumption of significant population growth. This is because the public pension fund is constructed based on a pay-as-you-go system; this system currently threatened by the serious crisis of the starvation of the fund. A huge amount of public resources is being poured to keep the system from collapsing. Therefore, some steady and incessant improvement in production is urgently needed.

While many researchers tackle this problem with the total factor productivity (TFP) analysis, it must be noted that TFP is a vague concept. Since TFP is measurement of errors of production function, it is difficult to understand the production factors that comprise TFP. Although TFP researchers stress the importance of TFP growth, this is cumbersome task because there is little information on the economic factors that affect TFP.

However, once one takes the inseparability of production resources into consideration explicitly, one can clarify one of the most important contents of TFP: management skills. To exhibit this assertion, let us return to the shape of the aggregate production function:

$$y = \psi\left(\lambda\left(e^{Nk}\left(y^{d}\right), e^{Nk}\left(y^{d}\right)\right), \lambda\left(e^{Nk}\left(y^{d}\right), e^{Nk}\left(y^{d}\right)\right), y^{d}\right), \tag{5.17}$$

where e^{Nk} is the Nash equilibrium hours-worked function, which is ranked the kth in the Pareto order.[17] Accordingly,

[17]For simplicity, we regard number of hours as a proxy of the employee's effort.

$$e^{*} > e^{Nk} > e^{Nk+1}, \quad \forall k \geq 1. \tag{5.18}$$

Furthermore, let effort level, which is assumed equal to hours worked, be an observable variable, and the efficiency unit of labor supply, L_i, be an unobservable variable. It is also assumed that an econometrician who estimates the production function Eq. (4.17) cannot find the change in the Nash equilibrium hours-worked function except for the initial location.

If the production function measured by the efficiency unit of labor is the Cobb-Douglas form such as

$$y = [L_1]^{\frac{1}{2}}[L_2]^{\frac{1}{2}} \cdot f\left(y^d\right), \tag{5.19}$$

taking the difference of Eq. (4.17) logarithmically, one approximately obtains

$$\frac{\Delta y}{y_0} = \frac{\lambda^{N0}\left(y_1^d\right) - \lambda^{N0}\left(y_0^d\right)}{\lambda^{N0}} + \left[\frac{\lambda^{Nk}\left(y_1^d\right) - \lambda^{N0}\left(y_1^d\right)}{\lambda^{N0}} + \frac{f\left(y_1^d\right) - f\left(y_0^d\right)}{f\left(y_0^d\right)}\right], \tag{5.20}$$

where λ^{N0} is the initial labor supply in accordance to a Nash equilibrium allocation. The first term of the right-hand side of Eq. (5.20) is the estimated total contribution of labor in the efficiency unit to the production growth, which is evaluated by the initial management skills. The second terms in the bracket correspond to TFP in this model in the sense that this term is not directly observed and defined by the measurement error. However, the economic meaning of this term is serious. These represent the contribution of the progress ratio of the management skills and that of the aggregate demand (the third term in the bracket). In this context, the management skills imply the measures that should be implemented to prompt coordination. As aforementioned, non-cooperate behavior deteriorates the efficiency within a firm, and hence coordination must be introduced through the inseparability of jobs. Essentially, as far as some part of the actual variation of TFP reflects the progress or digression in the management skills, recent studies on the Japanese TFP provides indirect but persuasive evidence of our theory: coordination failure is the prominent cause of the economic stagnation in Japan.[18]

5.5 Concluding Remarks

In this section, we analyzed the reasons behind the long stagnation and zero economic growth in the current Japanese economy. We advocate that zero growth would be inevitable sooner or later because the requirement of the sustainability in the economy, especially rapid reduction of carbon dioxide emissions is vital for

[18]For example, see Fukao (2012).

human beings. If this economic constraint becomes severe, then the Japanese economy will record a negative growth rate in terms of GDP per capita. In an attempt prepare for the future, the efficiency of economy should be enhanced significantly.

One must note that a zero growth economy does not imply a gray society. A zero growth economy would replace incumbent industries with new energy-saving industries keeping the total scale of economy unchanged or smarter. To realize such active metabolism, Japan should evacuate from the current entrapped situations.

First, the incautious surge of FDI should be restrained through a rational collective decision. This is not only because FDI deprives domestic investment and employment opportunities, but also because earnings from FDI remittance to headquarters in the home country are hindered. That is, the lock-in effect to remittance exists under the existing flexible exchange rate system, and thus, profits of overseas branches hardly enrich the domestic economy. Regardless of such distasteful investment results, firms are still eager to seek cheaper labor in East Asia. This pathology is due to fallacy of composition. FDI firms forget the following principle: although one firm can enjoy cheap labor force, this consequence cannot be applied when an entire industry takes the same behavior because of the appreciation of JPY. Therefore, a collective decision for controlling FDI should be vitally enacted.

As discussed in Chap. 4, Shimomura advocated the necessity of self-restraint concerning automobile export to the US in the first half of the 1980s. This is because he was cautious about the excess exports depriving employment opportunities of the American workers. At the same time, he asserted the importance of *discipline*. As the former chapter indicates, Shimomura (1987) defines discipline as a code of conduct: "each economic agent should think of the whole and control the self." In other words, discipline is a conventional wisdom by which people can avoid the fallacy of composition. Accordingly, Shimomura's thought is still applicable to the current Japanese economy, which is disrupted by the serious industrial hollowing caused by FDI.

The second economic flaw of the stagnant Japanese economy is the meltdown of the Japanese firm as an entity. According to Coase (1937), a firm solves what a market cannot solve. A market functions efficiently when labor as an input is divisible. In this case, a firm, or more generally, an organization becomes redundant. This situation is typically presumed by neoclassical economists. As shown in Sect. 5.2.1, deregulation in the Japanese labor market is enforced along this line of thought.

However, there is no denying that the range of jobs is overlapped, thereby blurring the boundary of jobs and the boundary blurs in reality. This fact implies that there is no defined job boundary and the overlapping description would allow an individual to perform functions of correlated coordination, which is the need of the firms in the current scenario. Therefore, the deregulation in the labor market that aims to facilitate FDI, lowers the efficiency of firms in the home country. In the 1980s, many Japanese firms succeeded in the internalization of the externality, which comes from the inseparability of jobs. Additionally, Japan enjoyed premature prosperity, while pecuniary abundance had triggered the bubble and its outbreak in the early 1990s.

The labor market deregulation, which started in the latter half of the 1990s, considers the coordination system in the firm and industry as a kind of adherence. The advocates insist that this system delays the recovery from the bust by hindering free labor mobility from the declining industries to uprising industries, at least at its face value. The consequence is that the contribution ratio of labor to the growth rate was almost negative or negligible from 1995 to 2013 (Japan Productivity Center).

As such, it is quite arguable that the positive aspects of the deregulation of the labor market exist. Besides the difficulty in passing on work ethics, which requires mutual and face-to-face communication, loyalty to a firm is segmented between the regular and dispatched employees. Loyalty sustains employee's belief that his job is socially evaluated through company, and strengthens the tiebond of employees with the company. To summarize, loyalty is a genuine device that promotes coordination behavior of employees. This can be economically viewed as an internalization of externality, which comes from the overlapping within a company. As precisely discussed in Sect. 5.3.1, it might be not too exaggerated to state that the deregulation of the labor market causes *coordination failure*.

In addition, the aggressive fiscal-monetary policy by the current cabinet has made matters worse. When there is no demand expansion, the curtailed profits give a true indication of management efficiency. Nevertheless, it would be difficult for the managers to capture such signal as management efficiency, to the extent that the expansion of the aggregate demand dominates the advances in the supply-side inefficiency. There is a vicious cycle in which the aggressive aggregate demand management enhances the deregulation of the labor market (i.e., the meltdown of firm as an entity), and vice versa.

Since such government expenditure is financed mostly by public debt, the tax burden is usually transferred to the future generation. In this sense, the aggressive fiscal-monetary policy is provocative and has an opium-like existence.

References

Coase, R. H. (1937). The nature of the firm. *Economica, 4,* 386–405.

Fukao, K. (2012). *The lost two decades and the Japanese economy (Ushinawareta 20 nen to nihon keizai)*. Tokyo: Nikkei Publishing Inc. (in Japanese).

Iwase, T., & Sato, M. (2014). Retained profits and profit distribution of the Japanese corporation from the view of financial statements statistics of corporations by Industry. In *Finance* (pp. 86–95). Tokyo: Ministry of Finance (in Japanese).

Otaki, M. (2015a). *The origin of the prolonged economic stagnation in contemporary Japan: the factitious deflation and meltdown of the Japanese firm as an entity*. London: Routledge.

Otaki, M. (2015b). *Keynesian economics and price theory: Re-orientation of a theory of monetary economy*. Tokyo: Springer.

Otaki, M. (2015c). Public debt as a burden on the future generation: A Keynesian approach. *Theoretical Economics Letters, 5,* 651–658.

Shimomura, O. (1987). *Nihon wa Warukunai (Japan is not to be blamed)*. Tokyo: Bungei Shunju NESCO. (in Japanese).

Yanagisawa, F. (2008). *Deregulation of the labor laws during these ten years*. Reference of National Diet Library (in Japanese).

Chapter 6
Sustainability and Corporate Management

Abstract We clarify the essence of corporate management, which is based on Dr. Shimomura's vision of a zero-growth economy. It is necessary to observe the three principles of sustainability in a zero-growth economy and maintain the social common capital proposed by Professor Uzawa in an appropriate state to maintain a sound world economy. Corporate management in the twenty first century should establish a clear vision for contributing toward the realization of a sustainable market economy. In Japan, corporate management is changing. Corporate social responsibility (CSR) is considered important for environmental management, and stakeholder management (SHM) or "Japanese management practices" are considered essential for developing competitive strategies. Recently there has been a convergence between CSR and SHM. In short, the corporate management division of leading firms is now integrating CSR and SHM. These firms are changing their strategy to realize the new vision of global sustainability. It can be stated that a stable and sustainable economy implied by Dr. Shimomura's vision of zero-growth will be realized through proactive and cooperative stakeholder management in visionary companies.

Keywords Environmental management · Japanese management practice · Stakeholder management · Sustainability · Visionary company

6.1 Zero Growth and Sustainability

6.1.1 New Problem

In 1990s, the worsening global environmental problems began to attract public attention; today, these problems pose serious social, economic, and political issues.[1]

It seems that environmental problems, such as global warming and reductions in biodiversity, have strengthened the foundations of Dr. Shimomura's vision of zero growth. It is forecasted that the global economic activities would be severely

[1]See Horiuchi (2008).

K. Horiuchi and M. Otaki, *Dr. Osamu Shimomura's Legacy and the Postwar Japanese Economy*, Development Bank of Japan Research Series,
DOI 10.1007/978-981-10-5762-5_6

restricted by the natural environment and consumption of fossil fuels.[2] In this sense, it can be stated that Dr. Shimomura also had the view and understanding of an environmentalist. We have to consider seriously the meaning of zero growth and apply this vision to public policy and corporate management. The vision of zero growth presented by Dr. Shimomura had profound implications for sustainable development, which we will examine in the following sections.

Around the first oil crisis in 1973, the visions of zero growth were published in the *Limit to Growth* by the Club of Rome and in *Small is Beautiful* by E. F. Schumacher. As environmental problems emerged, new ideas and analysis were presented, such as "Four System Conditions," proposed by The Natural Step (a Swedish NGO); "Factor Ten"; "Gaia Hypothesis"; "Ecological Footprint;" "Zero Emissions;" and the idea of a closed-loop society.[3]

The developed countries have apparently reached a stage of zero growth. Sustainability, instead of growth, has become the biggest agenda. In this context, it has become important to change economic systems of developed countries, such as mass production, mass consumption, and mass waste. In his vision of zero growth, Dr. Shimomura showed the direction of innovation that is necessary to establish a sustainable market economy in Japan, and The Natural Step clarified the concept of sustainability[4]. With these theories in mind, we should develop breakthrough technologies that will enable the economy to realize the goals mentioned in "Factor Ten."

Developing countries may proceed along a new path that is different from what developed countries experienced in the past. The international division of labor should be reorganized to ensure that the economic activities of each country are based on the principles of closed-loop and sustainability. People in developing countries can benefit from breakthrough technologies in advanced countries, such as decentralized and renewable energy and IT-related technologies. In this respect, Hart (2005) presented an interesting strategy of the large multinational corporations (MNCs). According to Hart, MNCs will find new business opportunities for corporate growth by meeting the needs of the 4 billion poor people in developing countries. According to his new business model, MNCs will contribute to raising the income of the poor and conserving the natural environment of developing countries.

6.1.2 Sustainability

According to Brundtland's report of the World Commission on Environment and Development, *Our Common Future* (1987), sustainable development is defined as

---

[2]Other sources of energy, such as LNG and shale oil, are being developed. Due to global warming, these resources should not be exhausted. In this sense, a limit of oil supply exists.

[3]During the Edo era (1603–1867), Japan pursued a national isolation policy. It is said that the Japanese people achieved a perfect closed-loop society during that period. That is, their lifestyle was compatible with the natural cycle. Everything was recycled. People cherished things and used them for a long time with care.

[4]See Robèrt, K.-H. (1994).

"development that meets the needs of the present without compromising the ability of future generations to meet their own needs."

In order to maintain a sound world economy, the Japanese economy and other developed economies should achieve stability and sustainability. Taking into account Dr. Shimomura's theory, the definition of sustainable development by the Brundtland Commission, and the theories and knowledge of natural scientists and economists, the economies of developed countries should meet the following conditions in a zero growth state.

<3 principles for sustainability in a zero growth economy>

(a) The economy should be in equilibrium on macroeconomic and microeconomic levels; this implies that it is essential to achieve internal and external equilibrium.
(b) Lifestyles and economic activities should be compatible with the natural cycle of the earth.
(c) Basic needs of an individual should be satisfied and well-being of an individual should not decrease across generations.

6.1.3 Zero Growth and Stationary State

A sustainable zero growth economy would lead the economy to a "stationary state," thereby fulfilling the vision of J. S. Mill. The notion of social common capital of Uzawa (1994, 2005) is essential for achieving Mill's vision. The social common capital consists of natural environment, social infrastructure, and institution. These are defined as follows.

<Social common capital by Uzawa>

Natural environment: It comprises atmosphere, oceans, rivers, lakes, woods, animals, plants, among others.

Social infrastructure: It comprises highways; ports and "lifelines," such as water, sewerage and electricity; and other networks.

Institution: It encompasses justice, public administration, finance and banking, education, medical care, corporation, among others.

Social common capital must be efficiently managed for establishing a sustainable and stationary zero growth economy. Social common capital forms the basis for the proper functioning of a market economy. Among other forms of social common capital, Uzawa pointed out that institutions, especially education and medical care, will be increasingly important for the sustainability of a society.

Social common capital is owned by both public and private enterprises, and people with special knowledge and competence are typically in charge of its management. Uzawa points out that it is necessary for these people to work according to their professional ethics. This also applies to professional managers of large corporations, because system of modern corporations is considered one of social institutions. While economic policies to maintain macroeconomic equilibrium remain important, public policy to manage social common capital properly will become increasingly essential.

Dr. Shimomura clarified his vision of zero-growth and emphasized the need for discipline on the part of economic agents. In the context of discipline, morality and proper management of social common capital would be essential for achieving sustainability.

We have not focused much on vision, discipline, and institutions, but these factors will be crucial for achieving sustainability in the economy. These factors will also be important for managing corporations in a sustainable society. Stakeholders, in addition to stockholders, will be increasingly important for meeting corporate social responsibility (CSR). In this sense, current practice of management to make too much of stockholders must be modified.

The Japanese economy is now at a great turning point. We need a new vision. This new vision will change the lifestyles of individuals and the style of doing business. It is difficult to change the present culture in a short-term because it is rooted firmly in our economic activities, but a gradual change is evident in advanced corporations.

6.2 Vision of the Corporation

The Japanese businesspersons did not understand Dr. Shimomura's vision of zero-growth partly because it did not refer to the vision of a firm. Dr. Shimomura was a macro economist, and he did not focus on microeconomic issues. Similar to the case of high growth, the vision of the corporation should be in line with the macroeconomic vision. The new vision of the corporation will be formed based on sustainability. In case of Japan, the vision of the corporation can be understood by looking at the history of environmental management by firms.

6.2.1 Environmental Management in Japan

1. Three Stages of Development

The first industrial pollution problem in the postwar period occurred soon after the World War **II**, in which cadmium (Cd) from industrial processes caused adverse effects on human health. In the mid-1950s, the drainage water from petrochemical plants that contained mercury (Hg) caused Minamata disease. In the beginning of the 1960s, polluted air caused asthma in industrial areas. In the mid-1960s, there was an increase in the number of hazards due to mercury pollution. These four industrial pollution incidents led people to file lawsuits against corporations and the government; the victims of these incidents won the lawsuits. However, the government was passive and did not take effective and immediate environmental measures. In 1967, the government introduced a pollution prevention law that was deemed insufficient, and it was revised in 1970.

In the latter half of the 1980s, new kinds of chemical materials began to attract attention. These were polychlorinated biphenyls (PCBs), dioxins, environmental hormones (endocrine disrupters), among others, which affect human health even in very small concentrations. In the 1990s, global environmental problems, especially global warming and losses of biodiversity, became the causes for concern.[5]

As mentioned above, in the 1960s, pollution began to pose serious issues. However, the corporations ignored these issues. In the 1970s, this problem became a very serious social issue. An anti-growth sentiment became conspicuous in the media and people argued about the need for corporate social responsibility (CSR).

The government, especially local governments in industrial zones and large cities, began to adopt very stringent policies to control industrial pollution. Regulation in the form of direct control was enforced. Monitoring systems of local governments were very powerful.

Large corporations, especially those in energy and material-intensive industries, were forced to make agreements with municipalities and observe regulations to get "a license to operate" as a going concern. This was related to whether a company could carry out investments continuously. Local governments represented their local communities. The firms were mostly reactive; additionally, interactions with the local government were not regarded as proactive stakeholder dialogues with a strategic management perspectives.

Environmental management was "reactive" and aimed at achieving compliance. In order to comply with severe restrictions, corporations developed technologies to control the sulfur oxide emissions and other hazardous wastes. At that time, the serious pollution hazards were controlled through technological developments. As a result, economic growth was possible. This is the main reason why we observed an inverse U-shaped relationship between GDP per capita and the pollution level. This tendency will not readily apply in the case of global environmental problems.

Direct regulations and technological developments were characteristics of such environmental measures. Corporations used "end of pipe" technologies, which increased production costs. Trade-offs between environmental measures and profitability were experienced, and managers were reluctant to take measures to control pollution. These trade-offs implied that the environmental measures did not address the root causes of the pollution problems. Therefore, innovation to realize a win-win solution was necessary. In the 1970s, firms invested actively in energy saving innovations, which improved profitability, controlled air pollution, and aided the mitigation of global warming problems. Energy saving will be a lasting challenge for industries. Innovations to reduce energy and material usage contribute toward profitability and the conservation of the natural environment.

Until the 1970s, corporations were generally "reactive," but there were some proactive figures among top managers. According to Miyakawa (1992), in the late

[5]See Horiuchi and Nakamura (2000).

1960s, K. Kikawada, CEO of Tokyo Electric Power Company and a representative of the Japan Association of Corporate Executives (Keizai Doyukai), expressed his view that a corporation becomes a public institution when control is separated from ownership, and that a manager in such an organization has to independently fulfill social responsibility by harmonizing the complex interests of stakeholders.

In the 1980s, environmental management reached the second stage of evolution. Corporations put more emphasis on the prevention of pollution. Environmental management became "precautionary and preventive," and measures were taken to reduce the amount of toxic waste produced during the manufacturing processes. Corporations improved their manufacturing processes to increase resource productivity. The objective of such changes was to reduce anticipatory environmental risks and contingent liabilities. The idea of "Pollution Prevention Pays" began to prevail among the industries.

In the 1990s, environmental management by leading firms became "proactive and strategic." Top managers began to realize that global environmental problems are not a threat but an opportunity for business. Environmental problems became one of the most important issues in competitive strategy. Corporations began to aim toward being the first mover who can enjoy learning effects and develop a good reputation in environmental management. Currently, the expenditure for R&D on environmental technologies is increasing rapidly and, in some major firms, exceeds fixed investment in plant and equipment. R&D is referred to as an investment in human assets, which is called "soft investment."

2. Environmental Policy of the Government and NGOs

The environmental policies of the government have changed since the 1990s. Direct controls remain for toxic materials. In addition, indicative and indirect policies such as standards, goals, and economic instruments are being introduced, and will become more important. These policies have clarified the direction of environmental measures and stimulated cooperative actions among corporations. For example, these policies have facilitated the recycling of household appliances and cars. Cooperative action is very important to avoid free rider problems. Members of industrial associations, NGOs, government officials, and researchers have begun to communicate and discuss policies. Meetings with multiple stakeholders have become increasingly necessary in the policy making process.

New environmental laws were stipulated to achieve a sustainable and closed-loop society. These reflected policies to encourage companies to reduce the consumption of energy and materials and promote the recycling of waste products, such as household appliances, pet-bottles, containers, cars, PCs, scraps from restaurants, and materials of demolished buildings. The concept of Expanded Producer Responsibility (EPR) was incorporated into governmental measures. An environmental tax (a combination of a carbon tax, subsidies for R&D, and investments to cope with global warming) was introduced in 2012. These measures may be insufficient and need revisions, but they will contribute toward improving the environmental efficiency in the long-term.

Global companies are becoming sensitive to new regulations in the European Union (EU), such as Waste Electrical and Electronics Equipment (WEEE) and Restriction of Hazardous Substances (RoHS). Efforts are being undertaken to harmonize environmental protection regulations.

In addition to the government, non-governmental organizations (NGOs) are beginning to influence corporate management. When environmental pollution aggravated in the 1960s and 1970s, NGOs and local residents protested strongly against the corporations responsible for the pollution. Currently, a new type of NGO is emerging. They interact with businesspersons and the government, and make proposals to improve corporate environmental management and government policies. Stakeholder dialogue is also becoming important for both corporations and the government.[6]

3. Environmental Strategy and Environmental Management System (EMS)

In the 1990s, corporate environmental management became proactive and strategic. Environmental problems became one of the important agendas in corporate strategy.

Today, strategic environmental management requires every section of an organization to take into account environmental considerations when it carries out its business. Therefore, environmental management systems. such as ISO14001, have been introduced by many corporations in Japan. Environmental management tools, such as Life Cycle Assessment (LCA), Design for Environment (DfE), environmental accounting, and eco-labels, are widely used by large corporations. To facilitate communication with stakeholders, many corporations are publishing environmental reports. This evidence suggests that large corporations are aiming for a win-win situation and striving to achieve higher eco-efficiency.

In the year 2000, corporations published sustainability reports instead of issuing environmental reports. Based on the notion of "triple bottom line," a sustainability report includes three things: economic (profitability), environmental, and social elements.[7] Social elements comprise labor conditions, product safety, philanthropy, contribution to the local community, human rights, sex discrimination, among others. Corporations refer to the guidelines of the Ministry of Environment and the Global Reporting Initiative (GRI).

Recently, it has been noticed that the top managers have begun to discuss corporate social responsibility (CSR) and the role of the corporation as a public institution. Managers did not focus on the subject during the 1980s, and the number of proactive managers that discussed CSR was small. The establishment of a

[6]NGOs in Japan are not as influential as the NGOs in Europe. This is one of the reasons behind Japan's inability to catch-up with other countries in some areas.
[7]See Elkington (1997).

separate business function for CSR, including environmental management, has motivated businesspersons to discuss stakeholder management.

To cope with global environmental problems, corporate management is being reformed. Discussions on CSR and stakeholder engagement have induced managers to think about the vision of the corporation.

At present, many corporations lag behind this trend. Even today, most managers tend to think that environmental measures are the use of end-of-pipe technologies. Since these technologies increase costs and reduce competitiveness, managers are reluctant to act positively. Generally, small and medium-sized firms lack the financial and human resources to take proactive environmental measures.

However, environmental problems are certainly changing the management of large corporations. Large companies are also influencing the environmental management of small and medium-sized companies through supply chain management.

Leading corporations are using proactive and strategic policies to survive as a going concern. Vision, strategy, organization, and corporate culture have become crucial for attaining success in environmental management.

6.2.2 *Corporate Management in Japan*

Organizational structure is important to carry out any strategy. In Japan, the "Japanese business practices" were formed in the 1960s. These practices were related to the organization of firms and contributed toward the realization of corporate growth. These business practices will be useful to achieve the new vision of the corporation in the twenty first century.

Under the Japanese business practices, corporations considered long-term relationships. In relation to employees, labor practices such as long-term employment, seniority wages, and internal promotion were established. Concerning suppliers, long-term transaction practices such as the *Keiretu* relationships were formed. *Keiretu* are long-term relationships between corporations, which is similar to the relationship between an assembly company and a parts manufacturer, and are intermediate transactions between an internal transaction and a market transaction.

These business practices were strengthened during the period of high growth of the Japanese economy. They contributed to the accumulation of firm-specific skills and expertise and enhanced collaborative risk sharing as a group. They were sources of competitiveness of Japanese industries.[8] Concerning the competitive strategies of corporations, employees, and suppliers were important stakeholders. At present, the stakeholder theory has begun to attract the attention of business

[8]In recent years, management of Japanese firms has been influenced by American business practices. The voice of stockholders has been strengthened and Japanese management puts more importance on short-term profit.

circles, in the view of a new vision in Japan. Focusing on stakeholders has become an important competitive strategy.[9]

With these practices, Quality Control (QC) and Total Quality Management (TQM) were promoted to improve product quality and the total factor productivity of corporations. The objective of corporations was to catch up with the advanced technologies of Europe and the US. In this way, corporate objectives and strategies were clarified.

The vision of the Japanese economy was rapid growth. The vision of the corporation was sales growth and profits in the long-run. The vision of the macro economy became the vision of the micro economy during the high growth period. The corporate vision was realized through the Japanese business practices.

Japan is now at a historical turning point. A new vision is necessary to form the basis of strategy, organization, and culture of corporations. However, the old Japanese business practices will be helpful in realizing this new vision, as we will see in the next section.[10]

6.3 Corporate Social Responsibility and Stakeholders

6.3.1 Three Basic Trends

As mentioned above, in Japan "corporate social responsibility (CSR)" was important for environmental management and "stakeholder management" was essential for competitive strategy. These two streams were independent, but they became closer and began to converge. In recent years, environmental management has converged with competitive strategy. CSR and stakeholder management will overlap and managers will integrate these issues to establish a new vision of sustainability. There are three basic trends that drive this overlap: environmental problems, globalization of corporate activities, and the IT revolution.

Environmental problems have changed from "local" to "global." Local communities focused on CSR and corporations developed technologies to reduce pollution in the 1970s. A specific section of a typical corporation was in charge of the environmental and social negotiations that took place with the local government and regional people. However, global environmental problems require corporations to adopt a different approach. They are directly related to the corporation's main business and involve every section of the business, across the value and supply chains. As global environmental problems became serious, top managers began to

[9]Due to the rapid appreciation of the yen and globalization of the economy, since the 1980s, some of these Japanese practices were reviewed. However, they are still important sources of competitiveness in successful Japanese companies.

[10]It is true that not many companies have a clear vision of the new era.

recognize the gravity of the issue and consider it strategically. They became proactive and strategic in the 1990s. Unlike the 1970s, managers should have a holistic view in the current era; additionally, we need more measures other than technological solutions. The meaning of CSR has deepened, and corporate stakeholders are expanding from local communities to the world.

Globalization requires corporations to consider the differences between their home country and host country. Direct investments of Japanese firms in developing countries are posing new social issues due to differences in culture and business practices. Social elements such as working conditions and human rights, which are important in the "triple bottom line" approach, are new issues that must be addressed. These problems are related to corporate ethics. The content of CSR is becoming extensive, and local communities and the government in foreign countries are becoming new stakeholders.

In addition, the IT revolution is promoting the connection of CSR with stakeholder management. Activities of corporations have become global, and information technology is advancing very rapidly. In this context, it must be noted that anti-social corporate behavior in a developing country will be criticized by NGOs, and this information will spread quickly around the world through the Internet. In Japan, due to business scandals, corporate ethics have become a focal point of discussion in the media. Corporations were forced to reorganize their structure and consider the influence of various stakeholders, such as whistle blowers, regulatory agencies, and the media, on their business. The IT revolution has enhanced corporate accountability to stakeholders, including the media and NGOs.

Environment, globalization, and IT revolution are the three main factors that promote consideration of CSR and stakeholder management by corporations. The content and definitions of CSR and stakeholder management are becoming important issues.

According to Post et al. (2002), a corporation needs to be redefined both conceptually and practically. They emphasize that the corporations are positioned in "the center of a network of stakeholders." They write that this stakeholder view is an extension of the strategic management theory of a resources-based view and an industry-structure view.

Freeman (1984) defines a stakeholder in an organization as "… any group or individual who can affect or is affected by the achievement of the organization's objectives." The corporation and stakeholders should have a common goal that is beneficial for both. This goal is achieved through the market mechanism and stakeholder dialogue. If corporate management is successful and the firm continues to operate in the long term, this will benefit all the stakeholders of the corporation. CSR is essential for maintaining the corporation as a going concern.

CSR and stakeholder theory are two sides of the same coin and have important implications for the vision of the corporation. CSR was the focus of the multi-stakeholders' meetings of the EU and the International Organization for Standardization (ISO).

6.3.2 *Fiduciary Obligations and Professional Ethics*

CSR and stakeholder theory apply to the management of large corporations. A large corporation has a significant influence on our economic, social, and cultural lives. It plays an important role in the workings of a market economy. Its governance is characterized by separation of control from ownership. Top managers, that is, the board of directors and executive officers, have fiduciary obligations to the corporation. They exercise leadership to fulfill these obligations and succeed in business. The corporation as a going concern benefits stakeholders whose goals are aligned with the organizational goals. In this sense, top managers of a large corporation have responsibility to stakeholders. This is what we call CSR.

When pollution posed a serious problem, Kikawada of Tokyo Electric Power expressed the need for CSR and set an example as a top manager. When the Japanese economy was in serious confusion after the oil crisis, Dr. Shimomura emphasized discipline that should be exercised by the corporate managers. Kaku (1997), the honorary chairperson of Canon, emphasized the moral duty of global corporations. He wrote about a business credo of "kyosei," which means a spirit of cooperation with stakeholders. A manager in a large corporation should behave according to professional ethics.[11]

In relation to this argument, global environmental problems have reinforced the role of managers. At present, global warming is damaging our life, and sustainability of the earth's ecological system has become a cause for concern for the public. Dasgupta and Mäler (2004) showed that it is important to take account of the irreversibility and non-convexity of ecological systems. These new studies imply that, in addition to public policy, professional ethics of managers will become more important for sustainability of the market economy. Global environmental problems are posing new challenges to managers. They should be aware of the results of academic research on the relationships between economics and ecosystems.[12]

CSR and stakeholder theory were originally normative, but now they are positive and practical. When we consider sustainability of our economy and society, we

---

[11]The following cases show that morality and professional ethics are important for business. Adam Smith is well known for 'sympathy' in *The Theory of Moral Sentiments*. The Merchants of Ohmi were wealthy peddlers in the Middle Ages in Japan. Their family motto was, "Be good to suppliers, customers, and society." E. Shibusawa (1840–1931) was a very active and influential businessperson at the beginning of the industrial era. He contributed to the establishment of about 500 companies. He emphasized two things: a businessperson should have a *sorobun* (a Japanese manual calculator that represents profit) in one hand and a book on the Discourses of Confucius (which represents morality) in the other hand. His motto was that business should be conducted in accordance with morality.

[12]See Berkes and Folke (Eds.) (1998) and Sundberg and Söderqvist (2004).

should focus on them as essential items on our agenda. They have a substantial influence on the strategies of large corporations in Japan, Europe, and the US.[13] A new vision is emerging based on CSR and stakeholder theory.

6.4 Visionary Companies and Sustainability

According to Collins and Porras (1994, 2002), a corporation which is successful as a going concern has a well-conceived vision. Vision means, "What we stand for," and it must be something that will last for a long time. A vision consists of a "core ideology and envisioned future." In relation to our argument, core ideology is very important. Collins and Porras define core ideology as "the enduring character of the corporation—its self-identity that remains consistent through time and transcends product/market life cycles, technological breakthroughs, management fads, and individual leaders." They insist that "the most lasting and significant contribution of the architects of visionary companies is the core ideology."

Collins and Porras explain that core ideology consists of core values and a core purpose. Core values are "the corporation's essential and enduring tenets—a small set of general guiding principles," and they form "the corporation's fundamental reasons for existence beyond just making money." Following their argument, core values and core purposes (long-term objectives) are two factors essential for the forming the vision of long-lasting companies. The product and services that a firm supplies are the means to achieve its vision. Referring to Collins and Porras, we will consider the ideas of core values and core purpose from the point of view of sustainability. This is because core values and core purposes are what we call vision in Fig. 6.1.

Österberg (2003), who had been chairperson of the Swedish Newspapers Association and a member of the top management of the Dagens Nyheter Group, expressed a very interesting view about companies. Looking at the natural systems, he realized that "everything is part of a whole and everything is interconnected." He concluded, "the primary purpose of a company is to serve as an arena or vehicle for the personal and human development of those who are working in the company."

The view of Österberg is very similar to that of the founders of Sony and Honda, and fits well with small-sized firms and new firms at their start-up stage.[14] His view gives a good example of the core values of a company. Core values are also very important in large companies. Collins and Porras summarize the core values of visionary companies, and we must understand that core values are often expressed in moral terms that include humanistic values, such as personal respect, the dignity

[13]Based on the principle of stakeholder fairness, Phillips (2003) clarifies that stakeholders are separated into legitimate and derivative stakeholders. The natural environment is not itself a stakeholder, but it influences a company through its stakeholders.

[14]These new start-ups will play an important role in bringing forth innovations. However, changes in large corporations are equally essential.

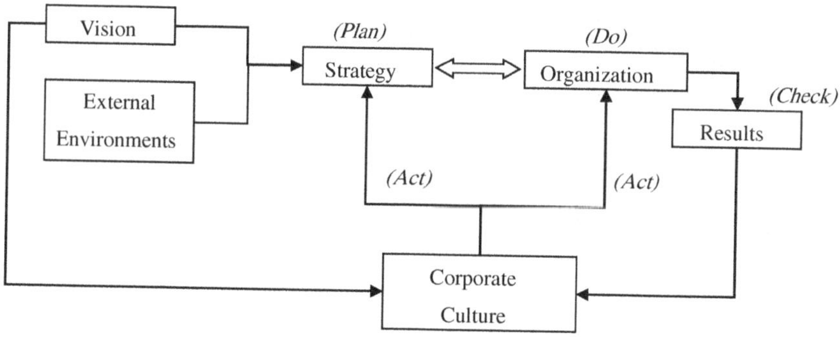

Fig. 6.1 Corporate management flow based on the new vision

of an individual, personal fulfillment, accomplishment, integrity, honesty, fairness, openness, creativity, contributions, and responsibilities of the community, among others. These core values are related with the ideas of "sympathy" of Smith, "morality" of Shibusawa, and "discipline" of Dr. Shimomura. Core values are the foundations for CSR and stakeholder engagement, and will be the most basic and long-lasting values for companies.

The core purpose (long-term objective) of a corporation reflects fundamental trends in the environment outside a corporation. Major movements of the market economy and society influence the core purpose. Following the argument of this book, the core purpose should relate to sustainability of the market economy and society in which the corporation operates. The core purpose of a typical firm was growth in the old vision, and it will be "sustainability" in the new vision.

As described above, history of environmental management in Japan shows that it was "reactive" in the 1960s and 1970s; it changed to "precautionary and preventive" in the 1980s and developed into "proactive and strategic" in the 1990s. Now, in the twenty first century corporate environmental management will be carried out to meet the vision of sustainability.

The transformation of corporate purpose from growth to sustainability will change the paradigm of the constituency of firms. People working in firms will reconsider the 20th century paradigm and look toward a new paradigm. A change in the paradigm will lead to a new corporate culture. This argument is important for large corporations that are very influential in the present society. A change in objectives and a focus on sustainability does not mean that a firm will not grow. A firm that contributes to sustainability of the market and society will increase sales and profit in the long-term.

Core values and core purpose are very important for a large company. The new vision defined above will stimulate new activities and innovation; additionally, it will offer corporations "a license to operate." We need innovation to change technology and management to attain the objective of sustainability. Sustainability requires managers to consider equity problems, which will influence the direction of innovation. This objective is closely related to the core values that emphasize morality.

At the beginning of the rapid growth period, Dr. Shimomura recognized that entrepreneurship was the main driver of economic growth. Now, entrepreneurship is considered critical vehicle for leading the economy toward sustainability. Corporations in Japan are now publishing an annual "Sustainability Report" in which top managers express their commitment to contribute towards sustainability of society. During the high growth era, the vision was clear and management focused on "how to do." Currently, "what to do" forms the focus of the firms. This is a challenging task for Japanese managers.

Strategy is determined based on vision. Management processes are carried out following the so-called PDCA cycle, which means "Plan, Do, Check, Act" (see Fig. 6.1). This adaptive learning process aims to improve performance continuously. As a result, corporate culture will change and move gradually towards sustainability. The vision of sustainability and process-oriented management will change corporate culture and improve corporate performance.[15]

6.5 Concluding Remarks

We have studied the macroeconomic history and business management in Japan. We found that vision is very important for stability and sustainability of the market economy and society. On a macroeconomic level, we should consider the meaning of "zero growth." Dr. Shimomura always focused on three basic factors: innovation, equilibrium, and discipline. The vision of zero growth will lead to the "stationary state" of J.S. Mill. We have pointed out that the social common capital of Uzawa should be managed properly.

The three basic factors that Dr. Shimomura emphasized are also important for management of the corporation, that is, innovation, equilibrium, and discipline. Using these factors, the vision of zero growth was linked to the vision of the corporation, and we could gain a deeper understanding of what Dr. Shimomura implied. At a firm level, we expect that large corporations should exercise entrepreneurship to direct the market economy toward sustainability. Corporate management is becoming proactive and strategic. These tendencies are emerging in leading corporations.

Stakeholder management will change. There are two types of stakeholder management: cooperative and non-cooperative. At present, the non-cooperative management is more evident. The interests of stakeholders are different and often conflicts each other. This type of conflict is often seen among workers, suppliers, customers, stockholders, and local residents. Stakeholder theory is based on the non-cooperative case. However, corporate management should change in a macroeconomic environment that is stationary and sustainable. To achieve sustainability of a society, the vision of a corporation should change thereby leading to

[15]See Horiuchi and Mukai (2006).

a change in stakeholder management. It will be cooperative, wherein all the stakeholders will share the same vision of a sustainable society. They will refrain from their self-centered mind and display a contented attitude. Stakeholders will be more cooperative. The cooperative stakeholder management is one of the examples of Dr. Shimomura's disciplines. Successful stakeholder management will be the main characteristic of a visionary company, which will drive market economy toward a sustainable society.

We must keep in mind that corporate management is not sufficient for the market economy to be sustainable. We also need to manage social common capital properly. Public policy to manage social common capital and proactive stakeholder management of visionary companies will move the market economy towards sustainability. The behavior of large corporations and the management of social common capital are two essential issues. These issues are not separate because a corporation or a system of legal persons is an institution, which is one of the legitimate components of the social common capital. Top corporate managers have a responsibility to keep this institutional capital in a proper state. Large corporations have become public institutions, and corporate management based on a new vision is required.

References

Berkes, F., & Folke, C. (Eds.). (1998). *Linking social and ecological systems*. Cambridge: Cambridge University Press.

Collins, J. C., & Porras, J. I. (1994, 2002). *Built to last: Successful habits of visionary companies*. New York: Harper Business.

Dasgupta, P., & Mäler, K.-G. (Eds.). (2004). *The economics of non-convex ecosystems*. Boston, MA, USA: Kluwer Academic Publishers.

Elkington, J. (1997). *Cannibals with forks: The triple bottom line of 21st century business*. London: Thompson.

Freeman, R. E. (1984). *Strategic management: A stakeholder approach*. Boston: Pitman Publishing Inc.

Hart, S. L. (2005). *Capitalism at the crossroads: The unlimited business opportunities in solving the world's most difficult problems*. Pennsylvania: Wharton School Publishing.

Horiuchi, K. (2008). A vision for corporate behavior under zero economic growth and global environmental constraints. *The Hosei Journal of Humanity and Environment, 1*(1), 1–22. (Tokyo: Hosei University).

Horiuchi, K., & Mukai, T. (2006). *Practical environmental management*. Tokyo: Toyo Keizai Press. (in Japanese).

Horiuchi, K., & Nakamura, M. (2000). Environmental issues and Japanese firms. In M. Nakamura (Ed.), *The Japanese business and economic system*. New York: Palgrave.

Kaku, R. (1997). The path of kyosei. *Harvard Business Review on Corporate Responsibility (2003), 75*(4), 55–63.

Miyakawa, T. (1992). *Corporate social responsibility and corporate ethics (mimeo)*. Kashiwa-Saitama: Reitaku University. (in Japanese).

Österberg, R. (2003). *Corporate renaissance: Business as an adventure in human development*. First published by Nataraj Publishing in 1993. New York: Paraview.

Phillips, R. (2003). *Stakeholder theory and organizational ethics*. Oakland: Berrett-Koehler Publishers.
Post, J. E., Preston, L. E., & Sachs, S. (2002). *Redefining the corporation*. Stanford: Stanford University Press.
Robèrt, K.-H. (1994). *Den naturliga utmaningen*. Stockholm: Ekerlids Förlag. (*Natural challenge*. Translated by S. Takami into Japanese. Tokyo: Shin-Hyoron).
Sundberg, S., & Söderqvist, T. (2004). *A survey of studies on the economic value of environmental change in Sweden*. Stockholm: Beijer Occasional Paper Series.
Uzawa, H. (1994). *Collected writings of Hirofumi Uzawa* (Vol. 1–12). Tokyo: Iwanami Shoten. (in Japanese).
Uzawa, H. (2005). *Economic analysis of social common capital*. Cambridge: Cambridge University Press.

Chapter 7
Conclusion

Abstract Dr. Shimomura was an economist as well as a theorist. He was famous for the dynamic growth theory, which was based on works of Keynes, Harrod, and Schumpeter. Based on his theory, he was confident that the Japanese economy would fluctuate but remain stable, and that it would attain high growth in the 1960s. In addition, he had a sharp insight into the future of the Japanese economy and presented us with two visons: high growth in the 1960s and "zero growth" after the oil crisis in 1973. Looking back, his visions provided a clear and correct direction of the Japanese economy. Once he expressed his visions publicly, he never changed them. He was determined and confident. He thought it very essential to maintain stability and equilibrium in the "zero growth" economy. He stressed that economic agents should exercise disciplines or self-restraint because the period of *laissez-faire* was over. He opposed the neo-liberalistic policies of the government and firms.

Keywords Vision · Neo-liberalism · Discipline · Global environmental problem · Sustainability

Dr. Shimomura (1952, 1971) was an outstanding economist in postwar Japan. His had a vision, theory, and policy that contributed to the high growth of Japan in the 1960s. He was famous for the National Income Doubling Plan in 1960. Dr. Shimomura influenced people, especially business leaders and managers. They paid attention to his writings in the newspapers and journals and listened to his open lectures in major cities.

Soon after the oil crisis in 1973, he changed his vision from high growth to "zero growth" (1–2% a year). This drastic change surprised people who could not understand his new vision. However, he did not change his logic. Cheap and abundant oil supply, which had been the basis for world economic growth, was no longer available.

His vision of zero-growth was accurate. If some special factors such as "intense-deluge" export, Reaganomics, and bubble growth are excluded, then the growth rate remained almost "zero," as pointed out by Dr. Shimomura, in the 1970s and the 1980s. A majority of economists ignored or overlooked this point and

K. Horiuchi and M. Otaki, *Dr. Osamu Shimomura's Legacy and the Postwar Japanese Economy*, Development Bank of Japan Research Series,
DOI 10.1007/978-981-10-5762-5_7

indicated at the success of Japanese economy in overcoming the oil crisis. Zero-growth vision has important implications for the current scenario and has an important meaning when we face global environmental problems. A zero-growth economy must be a sustainable economy.

From the 1990s to the present day, the Japanese economy experienced "zero-growth" and lacked stability and equilibrium. People referred to this period as the "lost decades." The labor market is one of the reasons behind the stagnation of the Japanese economy. The deregulation of the labor market caused the meltdown of the firm as an organic entity through coordination failure. Owing to this, management skills contributed little to economic growth. Additionally, owing to the inefficiency in the supply side of the economy, the Japanese economy witnessed a sluggish growth.

The growth-oriented industrial policy based on neo-liberalism produced poor results. For example, the deregulation of labor market in Japan stimulated FDI of Japan to Asian countries. A surge in FDI caused industrial hollowing, which might have threatened employment and macroeconomic stability. Firms may increase efficiency and survive global competition. However, it does not necessarily prove that Japanese economy completely stayed stable in a zero-growth economy. This case shows us a fallacy of composition.

The expansionary fiscal and monetary policies ("Growth Strategy") contributed to recording a slightly positive growth in the short run, but a slowdown in productivity due to loss of organic structure of a firm and rapid accumulation of public debt ensued, which would ultimately bother the economy in the long run.

Instead of neo-liberalist policies, Dr. Shimomura insisted that it would be important for consumers, labor unions, corporate management, banks, and government to exercise discipline. Additionally, he insisted that the consumers should be satisfied with current standard of living, which was at its historic highest. This self-restraint lifestyle depicts the Buddhist wisdom.

Firms should refrain from increasing the labor productivity. Dr. Shimomura was of the opinion that an improvement in productivity will increase unemployment in a zero-growth economy. However, in Japan, due to rapid aging and decreasing population, an increase in labor productivity and improvement of managerial skills will become necessary to maintain the pension system.

Concerning the addressing these economic problems, firms should develop a vision to achieve sustainability in a society and stakeholders should share this common goal. New approach based on new vision will realize sustainable corporate management. Cooperative stakeholder management is expected to replace current stockholder capitalism.

When banks lost self-restraint, we experienced a bubble economy. Therefore, discipline is needed in financial activities based on globalism, such as free capital movement across borders. Fluctuation and misalignment of foreign exchange rate disturbs the sound and stable activities of real economy.

The government should maintain the principle of balanced budget. Of the four disciplines, Dr. Shimomura (1987) was most concerned with the rapid increase of the fiscal deficit. Under a zero-growth economy, he opposed fiscal and monetary policies to expand domestic demand. These policies are not effective and are considered to increase government debt in Japan. This is exemplified through Reaganomics that started in the US in the 1980s. The US economy lost equilibrium on a large scale and suffered from twin deficits.

In other fields, discipline is necessary. Concerning international trade conflicts, it is necessary to adopt VERs to maintain stability in the economies of the trading countries. VERs facilitate controlled trade and is a way to avoid "beggar my neighbor" policy. Dr. Shimomura supported VERs and opposed free trade in a zero-growth economy. Free trade was effective when world economy had a strong potential for growth.

If Dr. Shimomura were alive, he would have opposed the surge in FDI in recent years. Japan is a populous nation and we have to be careful of industrial hollowing. He would have proposed a voluntary measure for FDI so that industries or firms concerned would observe self-restraint.

Neo-liberalist policies such as deregulation and globalization tended to increase instability in the world economy. Dr. Shimomura's insight into zero-growth economy enabled him to foresee this scenario. He emphasized that it will be difficult to continue with policies based on *laissez-faire* principles in a zero-growth economy.

The world economy will have to develop measures for solving global environmental problems. Besides, the Japanese economy is facing problem of aging and decreasing population. It may be conceivable that the growth rate of Japan will be lower than Dr. Shimomura's estimate of 1–2% growth a year.

Dr. Shimomura had a clear vision of zero-growth. In order to maintain an equilibrium and sustainability, we must recognize that disciplines or self-restraints are crucial. A vision of sustainability and disciplines that economic agents must observe will constitute the core of economic activities in a zero-growth economy.

References

Shimomura, O. (1952). *Economic fluctuation and multiplier analysis*. Tokyo: Toyo Keizai Press. (in Japanese).

Shimomura, O. (1971). *Options for Japan as economic giant: Collected papers*. Tokyo: Toyo Keizai Press. (in Japanese).

Shimomura, O. (1987). *Japan is not to blame. NESCO*. Tokyo: Bungei Shunju. (in Japanese).

Index

K. Horiuchi and M. Otaki, *Dr. Osamu Shimomura's Legacy and the Postwar Japanese Economy*, Development Bank of Japan Research Series,
DOI 10.1007/978-981-10-5762-5

The manufacturer's authorised representative in the EU is Springer Nature Customer Service Centre GmbH, Europaplatz 3, 69115 Heidelberg, Germany. If you have any concerns regarding our products, please contact ProductSafety@springernature.com

Printed and bound by CPI Group (UK) Ltd, Croydon, CR0 4YY
22/09/2026
02221059-0016